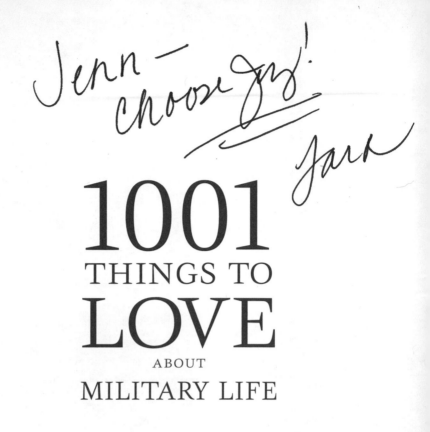

Jenn —
choose joy!
Tara

1001
THINGS TO
LOVE
ABOUT
MILITARY LIFE

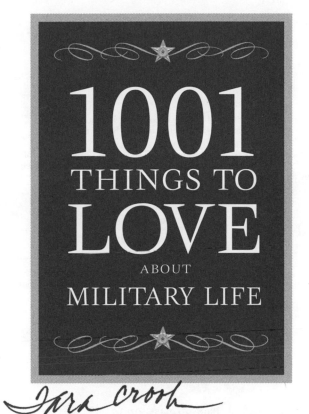

1001
THINGS TO
LOVE
ABOUT
MILITARY LIFE

Tara Crooks, Starlett Henderson,

Kathie Hightower, Holly Scherer

CENTER
STREET

CENTER STREET®

NEW YORK   BOSTON   NASHVILLE

Center Street
Hachette Book Group
237 Park Avenue
New York, NY 10017
www.centerstreet.com

Center Street is a division of Hachette Book Group, Inc.
The Center Street name and logo are trademarks of Hachette Book Group, Inc.

The publisher is not responsible for websites (or their content)
that are not owned by the publisher.

Printed in the United States of America

First Edition: November 2011

10 9 8 7 6 5 4 3 2

ISBN: 978-1-455-50283-7

We would like to dedicate this book to all military members and their families for their amazing strength and committed sacrifice.

★ ★ ★

CONTENTS

☆

INTRODUCTION

☆

When we first told people we were writing this book, responses ranged from "How can you talk about things to love with a war going on and military members being horribly wounded or killed?" to "Thank you for reminding us of all the good in the military and military life."

There are certainly a lot of things to not love right now about our military reality, as we continue into our tenth year at war. Military members and their families only make up one percent of the population but they are bearing one hundred percent of the sacrifice of war. The horrors of war, death, physical wounding, stress disorders and emotional suffering, and repeated separations, will impact our military families and society for a long time to come. War is hell. Even in peacetime, military life is constantly challenging.

However, research continues to show focusing only on the negatives can pull you into a downward spiral of despair and loss of hope. So, we decided to count the positives. The fact is, there are many things to love about military life. We really did not have trouble getting to 1001.

Our desire is that those of you who are or were in the military will read this—keeping in mind families and children serve too—and find yourself nodding in agreement at many of the items. Of course we know every example won't apply to every military member. Our military experiences differ as much as we do as individuals. We trust the examples we include will trigger your own memories and encourage you to share your favorites with your family and friends.

For those of you who are not in the military, we are confident this book will give you some insight into this military life and help you see why we have such pride in our military and lifestyle. Why we have not lost hope.

There is no greater love than a love that is willing to sacrifice or die, paying the ultimate sacrifice, for another. Our Service members love their brothers-at-arms and they love their country—freely and selflessly. Our aim is to help the country love back the same way, without reservations arising from the lack of an introduction to, knowledge of, or insight into our military way of life.

Ask any of us, "Knowing what you know now, would you choose this lifestyle again?'"

"ABSOLUTELY!"

We are grateful for the amazing people we've come to know in our military family and for the people we ourselves have become as a result of this lifestyle.

There are indeed 1001 things—and more—to love about military life.

★ ★ ★

Photo by Laura Fleming Photography

★

BE ALL YOU CAN BE
THE FEW. THE PROUD.
DO SOMETHING AMAZING
ACCELERATE YOUR LIFE
AIM HIGH ... FLY-FIGHT-WIN
THERE'S STRONG ... AND THEN THERE'S ARMY STRONG
BE PART OF THE ACTION
IT'S NOT JUST A JOB. IT'S AN ADVENTURE!
GET AN EDGE ON LIFE
A GLOBAL FORCE FOR GOOD
IT'S NOT SCIENCE FICTION. IT'S WHAT WE DO EVERY DAY.

★

WORTH JOINING FOR

*When I joined the Army, even before the turn of the century,
it was the fulfillment of all my boyish hopes and dreams.*

–GEN. DOUGLAS MACARTHUR

1. **The opportunity to learn new skills and gain experience that will change your life**

   *Recruiting slogans are created to show possible recruits
   things they can expect from a career in the military,
   but to us these slogans reflect the reality of military life.*

   –STAFF SGT. DAN MCINTOSH, U.S. Army recruiter

2. **Pride of service—becoming part of a team that values making a difference by serving others**

   *Ask not what your country can do for you.
   Ask what you can do for your country.*

   –JOHN F. KENNEDY

3. **Military Occupational Specialty (MOS), Air Force Specialty Code (AFSC), or rating—learning a skill that will transfer into civilian life**

4. Devotion to duty

It is not the critic who counts: not the man who points out how the strong man stumbled or where the doer of deeds could have done better. The credit belongs to the man who is actually in the arena, whose face is marred by dust and sweat and blood, who strives valiantly, who errs and comes up short again and again ... who knows the great enthusiasms, the great devotions, who spends himself for a worthy cause; who, at the best, knows, in the end, the triumph of high achievement, and who, at the worst, if he fails, at least he fails while daring greatly, so that his place shall never be with those cold and timid souls who know neither victory nor defeat.

–THEODORE ROOSEVELT, "Citizenship in a Republic"

5. Military leadership training, which is often "copied" in the civilian world

A good leader is one who causes or inspires others ... to do the job. His worth as a leader is measured by the achievements of the led. This is the ultimate test of his effectiveness.

–GEN. OMAR BRADLEY

6. The opportunity to live in foreign countries

Many Americans plan for years, often waiting for retirement, to take the "trip of their dreams" to Europe or Asia. And if they do manage to go, it's usually for a week or two, possibly three if they are lucky, racing around from site to site to pack everything they can into that short time. They create memories by snapping photos on the way to the next tourist attraction. "Photo op ... you have five minutes" is the common call of tour bus guides.

Compare that to the experience of many military members and their families. When you get to live in a foreign country for a year—or often longer—you experience that country in depth. Not only do you get to visit the country's highlights as listed in tourist brochures, you can visit these key attractions in off-season to avoid swarms of tourists. Plus, you get to live the life of the locals in many ways.

For example, living in Germany year-round, you can shop in the local butcher shops, cheese stores, and bakeries. You know when the farmers' markets start up and find your favorite vendors to return to each week. You can enjoy traditional Neu Wein, Zwiebelkuchen, and Spargelsuppe in spring and Kristkindlmarkts, Glühwein, and Lebkuchen in winter. Most important, you get to know the locals, learning about their customs and sharing your own.

What interesting foreign life experiences have you had?

7. A way up and out of a small town, big city, bad situation, or simply a rut

Eight years ago I was living in Philadelphia and I was not exactly heading in the direction I wanted for my life. A friend of mine told me he was going to join the Air Force and after he told me about the college benefits and some of the programs they had, I decided to at least go talk to a recruiter.

My first deployment cemented my love of the Air Force, and showed me that there are a lot of opportunities in my career field. So much has happened. I've been coined by two different Secretaries of the Air Force and dozens of Generals. I've helped with relief efforts ... Hurricane Katrina and the recent earthquake here in Japan. I had the opportunity to spend two years teaching combat skills to over 1,600 different Airmen across the Air Force who were deploying into dangerous countries. I graduated college with a bachelor's in Computer Science at almost no cost to me. The Air Force has been nothing but opportunities for me.

–SCOTTY D., *I'm Big in Japan* blog, MILBloggies' 2011
Best U.S. Air Force Blog

What is it like to be a military woman? ... It's like never being alone again in your entire life. It's having a family and discipline that your alcoholic parents could never give you. It's a chance for a high school dropout to turn her life around and make something of herself ... It was an experience I will cherish forever because the military saved my life and gave me the foundation that made me the person I am today.

–ELDONNA LEWIS FERNANDEZ, retired U.S. Air Force Master Sergeant
and coauthor of *Heart of a Military Woman*

8. Developing a work ethic and discipline that sticks with you the rest of your life

I was joining the Marine Corps for challenge and adventure, but everybody kept bringing me back to the fact that the Marine Corps was going to make you a leader ... It's about being disciplined, decisive, and ultimately it's about being authentic every single day ... Who would have thought the Marine Corps would teach me the skill set that would allow me to be a better parent, a better spouse ... ultimately, a better civilian.

–ANGIE MORGAN, entrepreneur and leadership consultant,
Captain, U.S. Marine Corps, 1997-2006

9. A higher standard

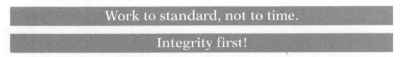

Work to standard, not to time.

Integrity first!

10. A well-respected profession

Gallup periodically conducts surveys to determine which professions Americans regard as ethical and which ones they don't. At the release of its 2010 poll, Gallup compared the results to those from 2004 to the present.

The professions that earn positive ratings from the public are, from top down: nurses, the military, pharmacists, grade school teachers, doctors, police, clergy, judges, and day care providers.

The group whose ratings with the public have risen the most? The military, at plus 8 percent.

When it comes to asking Americans which public institutions they have confidence in, the military has ranked No. 1 or No. 2 in Gallup's annual Confidence in Institutions list almost every year since the measure was instituted in 1973, and has been No. 1 continuously since 1998—higher than the police, the church/organized religion, the presidency, or the U.S. Supreme Court.

Gold is good in its place, but living, brave, patriotic men are better than gold.

–ABRAHAM LINCOLN

11. The opportunity to participate in peacekeeping and humanitarian support missions around the globe

12. Instant responsibility regardless of age

Where else can you fly planes, be the tip of the spear, and save lives, all at such a young age? One Coast Guard slogan says it best:

Born Ready!

13. Food and shelter

A single person who joins the military is guaranteed to have a place to sleep and food to eat. It's great for young men and women who may not have figured out how to budget their money. If they blow their whole paycheck in the first week, they can still survive.

14. Demolition

Certainly, one of the most thrilling experiences in a peacetime training environment is detonating explosives. That ranges from pulling the trigger on a bullet launcher, which sets off a controlled explosion in the chamber of a rifle or pistol, to initiating a blasting cap, which starts an explosive chain in demolitions.

One of the larger demolition weapons is the mine-clearing line charge, or MICLIC. Designed to open a vehicle-wide path through a minefield, it is a coiled, thick rope of explosives, which is carried over the minefield by a rocket.

Once launched, approximately a ton of explosives detonate at one time. Any mines in the desired pathway also detonate. This is a huge explosion, incredibly loud, with vivid colors, and accompanied by a powerful blast of waves that rocks even heavy armored vehicles.

–JACK SCHERER, U.S. Army combat engineer

Paratroopers from the 82nd Airborne jump from a C-141 Starlifter.

15. Flying

The thrill of flying in helicopters or jumping from planes. Need we say more?

16. Weapons training

Learn to shoot a .50-caliber machine gun, a main tank gun, a 40mm grenade launcher, and/or an anti-tank rocket.

17. Living your own boot camp or basic training stories

> *When I left Parris Island I walked tall, my shoulders were rolled back, head and eyes straight to the front, and there was nothing in the world I didn't think I could accomplish when I left the Motivated Island as we call it.*

–LT. COL. JERRY CARTER, U.S. Marine Corps, enlisted 1985, awarded a U.S. Navy ROTC scholarship, commissioned 1992

Photo by Photographer's Mate 1st Class Michael W. Pendergrass

Service members render honors as fire and rescue workers unfurl an American flag at the Pentagon following the September 11 terrorist attack.

18. The opportunity to defend freedom

People sleep peaceably in their beds at night only because rough men stand ready to do violence on their behalf.

–AUTHOR UNKNOWN

19. Developing self-confidence

Ben is a middle child. He was never needy, always quiet, not very social—very reserved. He wasn't outgoing, wasn't really involved in sports, but he was extremely smart. He always made straight As without even trying. He graduated from high school with no plans for college. Two years later his life was at a standstill, so he decided he would join the U.S. Coast Guard.

We were all very shocked and didn't like the idea. We were very unsure that this was the right path for him. But he always loved the water, boats, airplanes, and helicopters. (One time he saved a friend from drowning in a pool.) He ended up joining, and we supported him.

We think back on that day and wonder why we ever doubted such an intelligent, determined boy. We're so proud of him for joining the Coast Guard. It was the best thing he has ever done. It helped him become the man he was struggling to become at that time. It gave him confidence in his abilities. He was able to work with his hands in different areas, which fed his hunger for learning. It gave him a role of authority in his life.

*

The Coast Guard broadened his horizons by carrying him many places in the world that he would have never gotten to see otherwise. Now, he has many stories to tell. He also made TONS of friends—really military "brothers."

He has great insurance, benefits, and money for college. As a family, witnessing these things firsthand—all the changes he was going through—helped us to let go of him. We could finally let him become his own man. It gave us confidence in him, and we knew he was going to be all right.

–THE WILEY FAMILY

20. Getting your body and mind in great shape so you'll be ready to face any challenge that comes your way

... it [Marine Corps training] just gives you the mental toughness that it takes ... Anything can be accomplished with discipline ... I came in an undisciplined eighteen-year-old kid thinking I knew everything ... I left there a man with purpose.

–AHMARD HALL, starting fullback for Tennessee Titans, Sergeant, U.S. Marine Corps, 1998-2002

21. Making history while creating your future

22. A fast track to success

Male military officers are almost three times as likely as other American men to become CEOs, according to a 2006 Korn/Ferry International study.

> *I never heard anything at MIT or Harvard that*
> *topped the best lectures I heard at [Fort] Benning.*

–WARREN BENNIS, author and pioneer in leadership studies,
U.S. Army 1943-1947, awarded Purple Heart and Bronze Star

23. Finding out what you're capable of

> *Joining the Army was one of the best things I ever did.*
> *I was able to find out who I was. It allowed me to grow*
> *and become confident in my own skin. I gained confidence*
> *and pride in who I am and what I can do. Being a Soldier*
> *and serving your country is an honor and I was glad*
> *to be part of such an amazing institution. The best part*
> *is once you are in—you are always part of something*
> *bigger than yourself.*

–CHRISTINA PIPER, Army wife and military brat; her great-grandfather,
grandfather, father, and uncles all served; cofounder of HerWarHerVoice.com

24. A happy place to work

The headline hit the newswires and spread quickly in October 2010: "U.S. military beats out Disney as happy place to work."

CareerBliss, an online career-guidance tool, used 91,000 independent reviews to evaluate companies based on opportunities for growth, compensation, benefits, work-life balance, career advancement, senior management, job security, and whether the employee would recommend the company to others.

"It was interesting to see how well the military ranked relative to many top-tier corporations," said vice president Rick Wainschel. "After reviewing the comments from hundreds of reviews, it was clear our military Service members not only take pride in serving and protecting our country but find a deep sense of personal accomplishment in the important work that they do."

The Army and National Guard ranked Nos. 1 and 2 in the career advancement category, beating out Google for the top spots. The military also ranked high in growth opportunity, benefits, and job security.

Bradley Brummel, a professor of industrial/organizational psychology at the University of Tulsa (Oklahoma) and a member of the CareerBliss advisory board, added, "Despite challenges that may occur when serving our country, including the possibility of going to war, the military provides many of the essential elements to finding happiness at work, including having a meaningful impact on the world, having true camaraderie with your co-workers, and having the opportunities to develop skills."

25. Making something of yourself

You will become what you make of yourself. And it is that experience of being brought down to the common level, with everyone else, and knowing that everything you do from that point forward is something that you will treasure as your own. You haven't been given it. You haven't bought it. It hasn't been willed to you. You've earned it!

–ADAM FIRESTONE, Firestone Walker Brewing Company, Captain, U.S. Marine Corps, 1984-1991

26. ROTC scholarships

27. Paid-for education for certain specialties

The military will pay for education for those who wish to become chaplains, lawyers, optometrists, psychiatrists, dentists, physical therapists, physicians, nurses, and veterinarians. These opportunities are competitive and you incur an obligation of service, usually one-for-one for each year of education. You end up with your professional degree without huge student loans to repay, and you step immediately into work in your field inside the military.

28. Student loan repayments

29. The GI Bill

"A hell of a gift, an opportunity." "Magnanimous." "One of the greatest advantages I ever experienced." These are the voices of World War II veterans, praising the GI Bill, as reported by Suzanne Mettler, author of *Soldiers to Citizens: The G.I. Bill and the Making of the Greatest Generation.*

As she discovered from extensive interviews with GI Bill recipients, the educational opportunities provided by the program following WWII transcended boundaries of class and race, enabling so many young men to attain educational degrees and access to professions and opportunities they had never dreamed of.

GI Bill "success stories" abound, from former U.S. Senator Bob Dole to William H. Rehnquist, sixteenth Chief Justice of the U.S. Supreme Court.

Frank Lautenberg was born to poor Russian and Polish immigrants. After serving in the Army, he earned an Economics degree from Columbia University on the GI Bill. With two childhood friends, he went on to found ADP, one of the largest computing service companies in the world.

He later dedicated himself to public service, eventually being elected to the United States Senate representing New Jersey and now serving his fifth term. One of the programs he's helped champion is the modernizing of the GI Bill for military serving today.

[The GI Bill had a] transformative effect
on the lives of so many veterans like me.
    –SEN. BOB DOLE

30. The possibility of retirement at a relatively young age

*What made the military
worth joining for you?*

★

ARMED FORCES OATH OF
ENLISTMENT AND REENLISTMENT

I, (NAME), do solemnly swear (or affirm) that I will support and defend the Constitution of the United States against all enemies, foreign and domestic; that I will bear true faith and allegiance to the same; and that I will obey the orders of the President of the United States and the orders of the officers appointed over me, according to regulations and the Uniform Code of Military Justice. So help me God.

★

NATIONAL GUARD (ARMY OR AIR)

I, (NAME), do solemnly swear (or affirm) that I will support and defend the Constitution of the United States and the State of (STATE NAME) against all enemies, foreign and domestic; that I will bear true faith and allegiance to the same; and that I will obey the orders of the President of the United States and the Governor of (STATE NAME) and the orders of the officers appointed over me, according to law and regulations. So help me God.

ON THE INSIDE

~⭐~

SERVICE MEMBER

*History does not long entrust the care of freedom
to the weak or the timid.*

–GEN. DWIGHT D. EISENHOWER

31. Oath of Service

Everyone who enlists or re-enlists in the Armed Forces of the United States is required to take the enlistment oath. The oath of enlistment into the U.S. Armed Forces is administered by any commissioned officer to any person enlisting or re-enlisting for a term of service into any branch of the military.

The Officer's Oath of Office is additional to the Oath of Service and different for each branch.

32. Chain of Command

One great example of the Chain of Command in action is how Gen. Dwight D. Eisenhower approached D-Day. He had spent three years planning the invasion. On the day of, as Supreme Commander, he did not issue a single command. The plan and orders were in place, and it was up to those in the "chain" to execute and follow through. His job—trusting his men!

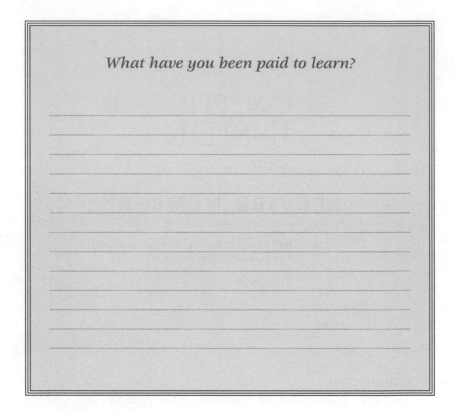

What have you been paid to learn?

DID YOU KNOW?

"Pilot" is the most commonly searched-for military career on TodaysMilitary.com.

33. Being paid to learn how to

★ Fly a plane
★ Rappel
★ Rock climb
★ Scuba dive
★ Jump out of an airplane

34. **Your day at the Military Entrance Processing Station (MEPS)**
Sweating the Armed Services Vocational Aptitude Battery (ASVAB), walking like a duck, and raising your right hand: all those things you did to "get in," "enlist," or "join up"

35. **Commander in Chief**
Knowing that our orders come through the people and Congress, and directly from the "buck stops here" position at the White House

36. **Being an unofficial ambassador for our country when living overseas**

37. **Being challenged to perform at your highest level, often way past what you ever thought you were capable of**

> *The difficult we do at once.*
> *The impossible takes a bit longer.*
>
> –U.S. NAVY SEABEES

38. **Standing in formation on returning from deployment, overwhelmed by gratitude ... and impatient to hear the words, "Fall out!"**

39. **Basking in your parents' pride and feeling like you've lived up to their expectations**

> *I was grateful to the Marines. I was watching my son grow and mature by leaps and bounds. I could only envy this great and life-shaping experience.*
>
> –FRANK SCHAEFFER, coauthor of *Keeping Faith*

40. **Greetings of the day**

41. **Crew cuts: flat tops, high & tights, zero-threes**

42. **Shower shoes, aka "Jesus slippers"**

43. **Hospital corners**

44. **Telling your neighbors you work at the Pentagon and they ask with awe, "What's it like inside?"**

45. **Setting a positive example for your children and "being their hero"**

46. Dream sheets and the anticipation of where your next duty station will be

POPULAR DREAM SHEET LISTINGS
(Assignment Preference Statements)

- **Anything in California, even Fort Irwin**—You can plan a picnic or a hike any day of the year because you know it's going to be a beautiful day for being outside.

- **Air bases, air stations, and Army assignments in Arizona**— For its lovely sunshiny temperate climate. With sunshine 85 percent of the time, it's even brighter than Hawaii.

- **Fort Carson, Colorado**—"Best Hometown in the Army"

- **Ramstein Air Base, Germany**—The biggest military mall and German beer

- **Hawaii locations—Joint Base Pearl Harbor-Hickam, Schofield Barracks, U.S. Coast Guard Honolulu, Kaneohe Bay Marine Corps Base**—Military, exotic destinations in the islands. Imagine getting orders to report there. *Oh darn! Not Hawaii!*

- **White Sands Missile Range, New Mexico**—Absolutely breathtaking scenes in your own backyard

- **Charleston Air Force Base, South Carolina, or Coast Guard Air Station, Savannah, Georgia**—"Southern charm"

- **Vicenza; Livorno, Italy**—Tuscany region, just minutes from Pisa. *Mamma mia!*

- **Nellis Air Force Base, Nevada**—*Las Vegas, Baby!*

- **Joint Base Elmendorf-Richardson, Alaska**—For its "longest day of sunshine"

What does your dream sheet look like?

47. United States Armed Forces Code of Conduct

*The name of American, which belongs to you,
in your national capacity, must always exalt
the just pride of Patriotism.*

–GEORGE WASHINGTON

48. Training instructors

All who ensure you receive the proper military training to advance
to the next level: Air Force military training instructors, Army
drill sergeants, Coast Guard company commanders, Navy recruit
division commanders, and the infamous Marine drill instructors
(DIs). If not for them, your preparation and day at MEPS would
be for naught.

Pressure makes diamonds.

–COMMAND SGT. MAJOR TERESA KING,
first female commandant of the U.S. Army Drill Sergeant School,
whose Soldiers call her "No Slack" and whose mission is
"teaching them how to bring troops home alive"

49. Fire guard

50. KP or Mess duty

Kitchen police—you either love it or hate it.

51. Chow

52. Chow hall, aka Mess hall, aka Dining Facility or D-Fac (D-Fack)

53. Knowing immediately what your "last four" are

54. Your unforgettable times in the squad bay or ready room

55. Pass in review

Your family may not pick you out of a crowd, but they'll sure try.

56. Guidon bearers

Straight and tall with impeccable military bearing

57. Skill training or Advanced Individual Training (AIT)

It's where you learn what you "signed up" to do.

UNITED STATES ARMED FORCES
CODE OF CONDUCT

☆

ARTICLE I: I am an American, fighting in the forces which guard my country and our way of life. I am prepared to give my life in their defense.

ARTICLE II: I will never surrender of my own free will. If in command, I will never surrender the members of my command while they still have the means to resist.

ARTICLE III: If I am captured I will continue to resist by all means available. I will make every effort to escape and to aid others to escape. I will accept neither parole nor special favors from the enemy.

ARTICLE IV: If I become a prisoner of war, I will keep faith with my fellow prisoners. I will give no information nor take part in any action which might be harmful to my comrades. If I am senior, I will take command. If not, I will obey the lawful orders of those appointed over me and will back them up in every way.

ARTICLE V: When questioned, should I become a prisoner of war, I am required to give name, rank, service number, and date of birth. I will evade answering further questions to the utmost of my ability. I will make no oral or written statements disloyal to my country and its allies or harmful to their cause.

ARTICLE VI: I will never forget that I am an American, fighting for freedom, responsible for my actions, and dedicated to the principles which made my country free. I will trust in my God and in the United States of America.

58. Mail call and mail drops

An AP photo in my local paper shows a Soldier, with a tank in the background, holding a letter to his nose. The caption reads, "Army Specialist inhales deeply before opening a perfume-laden letter from his wife." The photo tugs at my heart. The article goes on to say, "he ripped into it with an ear-to-ear grin"—one of the many happy Soldiers of the 3d Infantry Division, surprised and delighted by an unexpected mail call as they moved forward in Iraq.

Mail call. In today's world of instant messaging, cell phones, texting, tweeting, and electronic greeting cards, handwritten mail is almost an anachronism. But during a deployment, and especially in war, handwritten letters connect you to home and can be carried along to read and reread.

When my husband was deployed in Bosnia as part of the United Nations forces during that war, the only communication we had was very erratic snail mail—no e-mail, no Skype, no telephone connection.

I wrote letters every few days. And sent care packages. The writing was therapeutic for me as was putting together care packages, adding the strawberry Twizzlers and sunflower seeds he enjoys. I felt like I was doing something at least and connecting in the only way possible.

I remember vividly what mail call felt like when I was in my own initial Army basic training many years ago. The anticipation as we all gathered round. And the heart-centered tweak of exhilaration when you heard your name called. I can recall viscerally my sigh and quick turning away from the crowd when my name was not called.

I wanted my husband to be on the "got mail" side as often as possible during deployments.

–KATHIE

59. Standard Operating Procedures (SOPs)

60. Buck slips

61. Big black footlockers

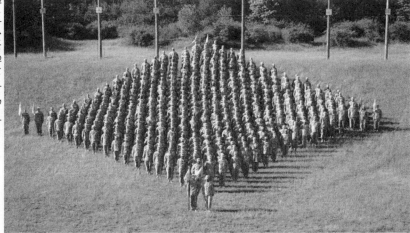

Photo by 1st Lt. Christopher Dunphy

Soldiers from Diamond Saber gather in a diamond formation at Fort McCoy, Wis.

62. Rank-and-file formations that are dress-right-dress

63. Military schooling—free training in marketable skills
You can come into the military with no training and they will train you. Very few civilian companies will do that.

64. Geographic Bachelor Quarters
Sure beats somebody's couch.

65. Staff duty
Extra great when you're on staff duty the night the XO's wife has a big party and you get all the leftovers!

66. Additional duties
"With great knowledge comes great responsibility."

67. Hand receipts

68. Preventative Maintenance Checks and Service (PMCS)

69. Safety campaigns

70. Stand-downs

71. Health and Welfare inspections

72. Barracks/dormitories

Barracks are buildings structured to be permanent military housing. Most commonly, "barracks" is defined as a building or group of buildings designed for the lodging of Service members. Barracks are typically found in garrison environments—in layman's terms that means that they are structures that reside on the installation (or with a permanent military presence nearby). Many believe that the original objective of barracks was to separate the Service members from the civilian population, thus reinforcing discipline and training. Barracks are definitely not the most elaborate of buildings. They are large, plain, and usually concrete or brick structures that resemble a motel or very simple apartment complex. This intent, combined with their distinct "look," earned barracks the term "discipline factories."

As times changed, there was a movement in military life that led to separate housing for different ranks and the development of married quarters. Thus, today, you'll generally find unmarried, junior enlisted Service members in the barracks as well as those serving an unaccompanied, dependent-restricted assignment; noncommissioned and commissioned officer ranks might also be required to live in barracks.

What is there to love about barracks? The fact that the military has provided housing. The housing is on the installation, which makes it convenient for the Service members to travel and utilize all of the installation services. Senior military members appreciate having all of their Service members in one area—sure does make it easier when it comes to training. But perhaps the most widely agreed-upon thing to love about the barracks suggests that the environment is similar to dormitory living at college—the esprit de corps and memories one builds while "roughing it in the barracks."

You Know You Are a Military Spouse When ...

You save an especially stinky shirt
to get you through a deployment

73. PTs—those smelly PT shirts

74. That regular physical fitness test ... an incentive to stay in shape

75. PT—"I'll count the cadence. You count the repetitions!"
    One two three ONE! One two three TWO!

76. Reflective PT outfits

77. Passing the fitness test—even better, getting a perfect score

78. Military tattoos—the skin art kind

79. Making weight

80. Post-wide runs

81. Rucksacks

82. Road marches or ruck marches

83. The honor of being a standard-bearer, akin to a "record holder"

84. Drill teams

85. Promotion points

86. Promotion boards

87. Professional development—formal and informal

88. Terrain walks—terrain analysis "on the ground"

Photo by Petty Officer 2nd Class Michael Hight

89. Being saluted

90. "I Love Me" books or the old "201 file"

91. "I Love Me" walls
Full of military guidons, poems, plaques, and photographs from units you've served

92. Getting "coined" by someone you admire and adding to your collection

93. "Attitude Adjustments"

> ### Pain is just weakness leaving your body!

Front Leaning Rest
Drop and give me 20
"Pound Sand"
GI parties
USN fashion shows
Smoke sessions

94. An outstanding evaluation report

95. Sergeants' time

96. Having "top cover"

97. Individual, collective, and virtual training

98. Obstacle/Confidence/Conditioning courses

99. Pull-up bar

100. Flight decks and flight lines

101. Being "volun-told"

> *If it moves, salute it; if it doesn't move, pick it up;*
> *and if you can't pick it up, paint it.*
> –ANONYMOUS 1940s SAYING

102. **"Man Overboard" drills**

103. **Slide for Life**
A three-cable slide from a tower to the ground, usually over a pool of water

104. **Temporary Duty (TDY)—an acceptable separation**
Relative to deployments, a six-week separation is short, no matter what civilian friends say.

105. **Operations Orders (OPORDs)**

106. **"Prior Proper Planning Prevents Piss-Poor Performance"**

107. **"If it ain't raining, we ain't training."**
In reality, it's the things like the unexpected—weather and otherwise—that make training "real."

108. **Basic rifle marksmanship training**

109. **The range**

110. **Field time**

> *No good decision was ever made in a swivel chair.*
> –GEN. GEORGE S. PATTON JR.

111. **Kevlar**
"Some people's heroes wear capes, mine wears Kevlar."

112. **SureFire lights**

113. **Clothing Sales Store**

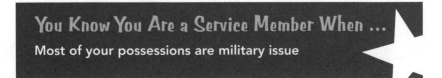

You Know You Are a Service Member When ...
Most of your possessions are military issue

Fort Knox by Paul Jon

114. Camouflage or war paint

115. Crooked-neck or L-shaped flashlights

116. Night vision goggles (NVGs)

117. Chem lights

118. Anything Gore-Tex

119. Silk-weight long underwear, aka "the Ninja Suit"

120. Polypro

121. Under Armour performance clothing

122. Poncho liners, fondly referred to by some as "woobies"

123. 100-mile-an-hour (mph) tape

124. Zip ties

125. 550 cord

126. Camelbak hydration system

127. Canteens

128. Rite in the Rain notebooks

129. KA-BAR knives

130. Camo netting

131. Water buffalo

132. Tactical or combat field gear—ammo pouches, first-aid pack, gas mask, and cat eyes

What are your favorite gear items?

Photo by Capt. Amy Bishop

Col. Michael Steele, Commander of the Rakkasans, 3rd Brigade Combat Team, 101st Airborne Division

133. Ammo boxes

134. Tents and tent cities

135. Concertina wire

136. Challenge and password

137. Navy or field showers

138. Clear skies

139. Call signs—think Maverick, Iceman, and Goose

> *I feel the need, the need for speed.*
> –TOP GUN

140. The feeling of freedom on that first jump out of the plane and the rush as you pray the chute will open

141. Coming out of the field earns a cold beer, hot chow at home, long hot showers, and rest

142. The salt spray on your face as the ship speeds through the water

143. The beauty of a sunrise or sunset from a naval ship at sea, and the beauty of the stars at sea

> *Benji often talks about how pretty the sunsets are on the boat when he is out for three months at a time. Also, about how they've watched movies on the deck while the sun was setting on the Caribbean and how beautiful the stars were.*
> –THE WILEY FAMILY

144. Mobile kitchen trailers (MKTs)—meals on wheels

145. Meals Ready to Eat (MREs) and A-rations
- MREs—Got to love them with nicknames like "Mr. E" (mystery) and "meals rejected by everyone"
- A-rations—Commonly known as "bag nasty" boxed meals by the Marines

What is your favorite MRE and why?

PVT Murphy's Law by Mark Baker

(C) M. Baker 2003

You Know You Are a Service Member When ...

You keep a box of MREs at home and in the trunk of your car in case of emergency

146. Home port and being homeported

147. Mandatory "fun"

148. Noncommissioned officer (NCO) calls

149. Officer calls

150. The "fun" of measuring exactly where to put your brass on your uniform and hoping the holes from the last time survived dry cleaning to make it easier for you

151. Shiny brass

152. Spurs and Stetsons

153. The humor that ranks combined with certain names results in—Major Payne, Major Minor

> Some Soldiers have the right name for the job. Who better than Chaplain Hart to spread the gospel message of love and forgiveness? There was also a Chaplain Meek, who was destined to inherit the earth. Once I met Private Love, who was, of all things, a chaplain's assistant. He and his buddy, Private Eye, couldn't wait to get promoted because they were sick of all the smart comments. You just can't make this stuff up.
>
> – MARNA A. KRAJESKI, *Household Baggage: The Moving Life of a Military Wife.* (For a very funny essay on this subject, read the entire chapter "Major Major" in Krajeski's book.)

> Our friend Heino Klinck. Ever since he made Colonel ... he's probably ribbed to death: Colonel Klink, "I know nosink, nosink." And in my basic Quartermaster Course, we had a guy named Bowe, whose first name was Colonel. So, as a lieutenant he could truthfully introduce himself as Lieutenant Colonel Bowe.
>
> –KATHIE

Photo by Sgt. Mike Macleod

154. Looking at the view out the open door of a helicopter

155. Gig lines

> We always told our husbands it wasn't fair. They had it so much easier using the gig line to line up all their uniform items and get things pinned in the right places. When we used the same gig line and then put on our uniform jackets, very often our body shape threw off the correct placement and we had to eyeball everything again with the jacket on. Not so easy or exact.
>
> –KATHIE AND STAR

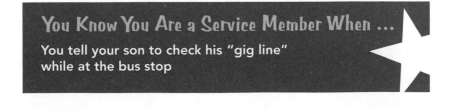

You Know You Are a Service Member When ...

You tell your son to check his "gig line"
while at the bus stop

Photo by Libby Conger

Officers and spouses dressed up for a battalion dinner and dance—part of our military tradition

156. Seeing the ladies "dressed to the nines" more often than you would in civilian life (at the balls and dining-outs)

157. Dining-in or Mess Night humor and shenanigans

158. The humor that arises from certain titles

> *Rear Admiral: Official title given to backseat drivers in the Navy*
>
> –LIFE MAGAZINE

> I always loved introducing my husband when he was the Professor of Military Science, the title for those in charge of ROTC programs at universities. "Meet my husband, Mr. PMS."
>
> –KATHIE

159. Learning to think "outside the box" as circumstances change

It's almost funny. So many civilians think of the military as being rigid, inflexible, and trained only to follow orders. The reality is that in wartime especially, as circumstances change constantly, you have to be able to think on your feet and find solutions quickly.

Our wars in Iraq and Afghanistan present an example. In countries where women are so segregated from men, the U.S. military has had to find new ways to interact with the Iraqi and Afghan women. It's something the male military members cannot do because it's wrong in the Iraqi and Afghan cultures for unrelated men to even look at the women, much less engage them in conversation.

One innovative approach, begun by the Marines and adopted by all the services, is the Female Engagement Teams or FETs. A typical FET numbers from two to four female military members, though they can be larger depending on the mission. These teams of female military members get permission from the male elders in a village or area to communicate with the women, asking what they need, providing help and resources.

One Marine FET in the Nawa District of Afghanistan, for example, has convinced locals to start girls' schools, helped the women start their own poultry businesses, and provided sewing equipment to communities, so the women can sell clothes to increase their families' incomes.

As Marine Corporal Sara Bryant said in a *Marine Corps Times* article, "Fifty-one percent of the population in Afghanistan is women. These teams are just another foot in the door to prove to them that we're not there to be an occupying force, but that we're there to rid that country of the Taliban." Plus, the women have such an important influence on their children, at least into their teens, so their views will greatly affect future relations.

The FETs are one way to reach out to Afghan communities in a culturally sensitive way. And just one example of how the military adjusts to conditions, finding new solutions for new problems. Not rigid at all.

* *

Education Support

160. DANTES—Defense Activity for Non-Traditional Education Support

161. Servicemembers Opportunity Colleges (SOC)
For both military members and their spouses, to help make a "traveling" degree program possible. The 1,900 schools offer reduced academic residency requirements, credit for non-traditional learning, and reasonable transfer of credit with minimal duplication of courses, so you don't have to constantly start over as was so often the case in years past.

See www.soc.aascu.org.

162. Tuition assistance for the Service member, even for graduate degrees

163. College credit for military experience

164. Distance learning courses

165. Community College of the Air Force

166. Foreign language training via Rosetta Stone—free for Soldiers and Airmen, reimbursable in many other cases

* *

167. Holistic fitness as modeled by the Air Force and Army with the Comprehensive Soldier/Airman Fitness programs

If one good thing has come out of these long years of war, it's the military's realization that our military members need holistic training for wartime and post-war.

> *As people develop their holistic fitness strength, they develop psychological resilience not only to bounce back, but to thrive under challenging conditions.*
>
> –BRIG. GEN. RHONDA CORNUM, Director, Comprehensive Soldier Fitness

168. Getting a great sponsor at your next duty station

169. In-processing, or maybe out-processing

170. Instant connection with a prospective/new boss, like a fraternity

171. Office calls to meet the boss, discuss your future, be mentored

172. Open-door policy

173. Service members who step up to advocate for change when needed

Some examples: implementing or bolstering programs for veterans or wounded warriors, lobbying for streamlined PTSD claims handling, and initiating Agent Orange research.

174. Military Outstanding Volunteer Service Medal

Awarded to members of the Armed Forces of the United States who, subsequent to December 31, 1992, performed outstanding volunteer community service of a sustained, direct, and consequential nature. Service member must be performing services on a voluntary basis, not detailed or tasked.

175. Short days

Commanders' time
59 minutes
Sustainment time
Family time

You Know You Are a Service Member When ...
You've given your children an "Article 15"

176. Uniform Code of Military Justice (UCMJ)
Order and discipline that all Service members adhere to

177. Saving money on auto repairs by doing it yourself at auto shops on the military installations

178. Vehicle discounts
- **Exchange new car sales**—Including Harley-Davidson motorcycles!
- **GM**—The Best Damn Military Discount
- **USAA Auto Circle**

179. Judge Advocate General (JAG) legal assistance—free wills and other legal advice and services

180. The Servicemembers Civil Relief Act
According to USAA financial planner J. J. Montanaro, the origin of today's Servicemembers Civil Relief Act (SCRA) can be traced back to the Civil War, when Congress first sought to protect the rights of those serving in the military. The law provides valuable, wide-ranging protection, including the ability to stay court proceedings, cap loan interest rates, and terminate leases upon deployment or Permanent Change of Station. What's not to love about that?

In fact, the daily news carries proof of the importance of the SCRA: In May 2011, two mortgage-servicing companies agreed to pay more than $20 million to approximately 160 victims of illegal home foreclosures on military members. The companies settled to resolve allegations by the Justice Department that they were in violation of the SCRA.

181. Family Care Plans—make you think and plan ahead

182. Medevac

183. Field medicine

Military doctors and technicians perform miracles regularly and develop new lifesaving techniques often in battlefield experiences.

184. Military members and veteran bloggers who share their war stories and experiences

We couldn't begin to list them all, so here are some favorites:

- *A Soldier's Perspective* militarygear.com/asp
- *Blackfive* www.blackfive.net
- *Bouhammer* www.bouhammer.com
- *Chief Wiggles* www.chiefwiggles.com
- *I'm Big in Japan* afscottd.blogspot.com
- *Military Money Might* www.militarymoneymight.com
- *One Marine's View* onemarinesview.com
- *Our Letters to You* militaryblog.militaryavenue.com
- *The Sergeants Buzz* www.thesergeantsbuzz.blogspot.com

What are your favorite milblogs?

185. Milblogging.com

A daily snapshot of the top milblogs, milblogs by country, and other cool stuff in the military blogosphere

186. Pinups

What does the word "pinup" bring to mind? A WWII sailor lying on his bunk looking up at a photo of Marilyn Monroe ... or maybe a photo of his girlfriend back home ... pinned up on the bunk above his head?

That kind of image inspired Gina Elise to start her "Pin-Ups for Vets" calendar project to raise funds to support all of our hospitalized veterans:

> *"My late Grandpa Lou served in the army for four years during World War II," says Gina. "I wanted to do something to honor his name. I always loved the romance of those bygone eras—especially the 1940s—and I drew inspiration from the World War II pinup girls, whose photos and paintings boosted morale for our Soldiers fighting overseas."*

She re-created a nostalgic pinup calendar to raise funds for our hospitalized veterans, as well as to deliver as gifts to injured veterans and to send to deployed troops. This award-winning nonprofit organization has been featured in *Stars & Stripes* newspaper and *American Legion Magazine*.

She has created five calendars to date. As of the end of 2010, she'd donated $50,000 to rehab programs for military and VA hospitals, traveled all around the United States to military and VA hospitals to deliver donated calendars herself, visited vets and wounded warriors at their bedsides to put a smile on their faces and thank them for their service, and sent hundreds of calendars overseas to deployed military to boost troop morale.

To see the impact of her work, watch the *Pay It Forward* video on her website at www.pinupsforvets.com/payitforward.html.

187. "Work Ups" or exercises

- **U.S. Air Force Weapons School**—Nellis Air Force Base, Nevada
- **National Training Center (NTC)**—Fort Irwin, California
- **U.S. Marine Corps Mountain Warfare Training Center**—Pickel Meadow, California
- **Joint Readiness Training Center (JRTC)**—Fort Polk, Louisiana
- **Marine Aviation Weapons & Tactics Squadron**—Marine Corps Air Station Yuma, Arizona
- **Combat Maneuver Training Center (MTC)**—Hohenfels, Germany
- **U.S. Army Combat Support Training Center (CSTC)**—Fort Hunter Liggett, California
- **Combined Arms Training Center**—Camp Fuji, Japan
- **Great Lakes Naval Training Center**—N. Chicago, Illinois
- **U.S. Coast Guard Training Center**—Yorktown, Virginia
- **Naval Strike and Air Warfare Center, aka TOPGUN**—Naval Air Station Fallon, Nevada

Which ones have you been to?

_____

_____

_____

_____

_____

188. Military online forums and how they help you connect and deal with the rigors of military life through shared experiences

189. The unique experience of eating local foods

What a great way to expand your culinary appetites! Chow abroad can be better than what you get in garrison back home.

★ Afghan kabobs
★ German beer and bratwurst
★ Iraqi meat and rice with baklava dessert
★ Japanese onigiri
★ Korean kimchi and bulgogi

> Through my career I've had many odd experiences with local foods, from eating blubber and blueberries in an Indian (Eskimo) village up north of the Arctic Circle in Alaska to eating live fish in Korea. I think the oddest foods I've felt obligated to eat were in the Middle East.
>
> We've all heard stories about being offered sheep's eyes as a delicacy in the Middle East, but in all of my times with the Saudis at various feasts and gatherings, I've never seen it. It probably dates from T. E. Lawrence's time or is something Richard Burton made up. At all of the gatherings I've been to, the eyeballs have stayed firmly in the sheep or goat with no one taking a bite.
>
> One experience took place in Taif in the western region of Saudi Arabia. I was visiting our U.S. advisors and coordinating training with the Saudi infantry brigade garrisoned there. Prince Turki was the brigade commander of the unit and invited me to experience a day "doing the Bedouin thing." We rode camels in the desert and then milked the camels and drank the milk directly from the bowl. It is quite a manly thing to do and as Prince Turki told me, it supposedly puts steel in the old rod (better than Viagra).
>
> Afterward we had a kabsa and ate goat, lamb, and camel. For dessert, Prince Turki offered fresh goat cheese in milk with dates. I cannot stand goat cheese but felt obligated to accept this delicacy, swallowing politely and struggling not to heave it back out.
>
> Back in Riyadh I ran into the personal physician for King Abdullah, then the Crown Prince. I knew the doctor slightly as we had worked on some projects together. When he heard that I had been out with Prince Turki and drank fresh camel's milk and ate

fresh goat cheese, he got annoyed. He told me I needed to go into the Saudi clinic and get checked out for brucellosis, an infectious disease that can last for years. So a few more times over the next year or so, I had to go into their clinic to get checked out and make sure I had not come down with brucellosis.

Foreign foods can offer more than a new experience. So far I've lucked out.

–MARK, U.S. Army

190. Having inexpensive shoes and clothes made to order in Korea

191. Thirty days' leave every year

192. Payday and payday activities

193. Calls and responses

CALL	RESONSE
"Blue Babe Sir"	"Strength and Courage"
"Airborne"	"All the Way!"
"Strength Starts Here"	"Army Strong!"
"America's Corps"	"Courage!"
"The Nation's Academy"	"Duty, Honor, Country!"
"Duty First"	"Service Always!"
"Climb to Glory"	"To the Top!"

What is your favorite call and response?

★ ★

Military Pay and Perks

194. Department of Finance and Accounting Services (DFAS), aka Finance—as long as they're disbursing, not collecting

195. Advance pay

196. Casual pay

197. Travel pay

198. Flight pay

199. Pay raises

200. Clothing allowance

201. Cost of living allowance (COLA)

202. Temporary lodging allowance (TLA)

203. Tax-free income overseas

204. Family separation allowance (FSA)

205. Dislocation entitlements

206. Thrift Savings Plan (TSP)

★ ★

207. Chiropractic and occupational therapy care

208. Payday loans

209. Joint domicile

210. U.S. Special Operations Forces
- Air Commandos
- Green Berets
- Night Stalkers
- Rangers
- Deployable Operations Group (DOG)
- SEALs
- Silent Warriors Raiders

211. Fighter pilots and crew chiefs—throttle jockeys and wrench turners

212. Strategic and tactical air power

213. Safety briefings

214. PowerPoint presentations
Sometimes "death by PowerPoint"—but no one can do PowerPoint like the military!

215. Training as you fight

216. Mine-resistant, ambush-protected (MRAP) vehicles

217. Deployment experiences between missions
Growing grass near the hootch, brushing your teeth in a sandstorm, getting to preview upcoming blockbusters before everyone back home, working with local nationals

218. SAPI (Small Arms Protective Insert) Plates
Every Service member issued one knows that the SAPI plate will save his or her life

219. Grenades

Courtesy Jeff Bacon and Broadside Cartoons

220. Briefings

*No grand idea was ever born in a conference,
but a lot of foolish ideas have died there.*

–F. SCOTT FITZGERALD

221. Creative training aids
Like the deck of "Most Wanted" terrorist playing cards

222. The adrenaline rush of training hard and having it pay off in combat

223. Combat camera
Prepared to deploy to the most austere operational environments at a moment's notice in order to capture still and motion imagery of our military in action

224. Combat artists—an official position in the military since 1917

225. Sharing "war stories"

All right, they're on our left, they're on our right, they're in front of us, they're behind us ... they can't get away this time.

– LT. GEN. LEWIS BURWELL "CHESTY" PULLER,
U.S. Marine Corps, most decorated Marine in history

226. Replenishment at sea or being resupplied on the battlefield

227. Eating great home-cooked food on duty days on the ship, because the supply chiefs got together and tried to outshine each other

228. Port calls

Ben was stationed in Charleston on boat number 721. The boat would go out for three months and come back in for three months. Those three months seemed like three years sometimes. One time, while they had been out for two months, they decided to dock in Florida on their way back to Charleston, South Carolina. So, my family and I "booked it" down to Florida with HUGE picnic "fixings" that included baked ham, potato salad, sweet tea, and everything that went with it. We met at a park that was very close to the military base. Ben packed as many friends as he could into a van and met us there. It was such a sweet moment when we all got out of our vehicles and hugged everybody, including my brothers' friends whom we had never met. I'm sure they thought we were crazy as we hugged them and cried on their shoulders just like we did his. Ha-ha! This was the very first time we felt that closeness to the military. It became more real after we sat and ate and heard stories of how they took care of each other. It was such a special day for us!

–ERIN WILEY, the Coastie's sister

229. Hooah!!!! Radio—Bridging the Gap 24-7/365, One Song at a Time

Visit the website to see how to become a DJ!
www.hooahradio.com

230. Proper load planning

★ ★

Teamwork
Together Everyone Achieves More

231. Civilian components supporting the military
- Civil Air Patrol
- Coast Guard Auxiliary
- Naval Fleet Auxiliary Force
- Merchant Marines
- Military Auxiliary Radio System

232. Allies

233. Reinforcements

234. Contractors

235. Interpreters

236. Military convoys—there's safety in numbers

237. Military working dogs

Photo by Gunnery Sgt. Bryce Piper

★ ★

238. Care packages from your family

CARE PACKAGES

Toothpick: To help you pick out the good in every situation you encounter.

Hershey's Hugs & Kisses: Because sometimes we all need a "hug and kiss."

Paper clip: To help you "keep it together" when it all seems to be hitting the fan.

Marble: To replace "the ones we all lose" from time to time.

Snickers: To remind you to "laugh" even when you feel like crying.

Rubber band: To help you be flexible and "bounce back" without breaking in times of trouble.

Stick of gum: To remind you to "stick" with the task at hand.

Mint: To let you know you're worth a "mint" to me.

Cotton ball: To help "cushion" the rough times.

Lollipop: To help you "lick" the problems you encounter.

Starburst: To let you know I'm "bursting" with pride for you.

Nut: To remind you to relax and get a little "nutty" sometimes.

Tootsie Roll: To remind you of the important "role" you play.

Life Savers: To signify the "lifesaving" things you do to keep our country free.

What is your favorite care package item?

Photo by Lance Cpl. Saulisbury

Tucked inside this little bag,
If your spirits start to sag,
Are little reminders that I care,
As you fight for freedom over there.

239. Letters from home

240. FamilyGrams

241. MotoMail

242. Listening to supportive and educational talk radio shows
   - *You Served* www.youservedradio.com
   - *Talking with Heroes* www.talkingwithheroes.com

243. Morale calls home

244. Downrange Internet cafés

245. Successfully timing a phone call or webcam date so that you can listen in on your baby being born back in the States

246. Deployment money

247. Military Savings Deposit Program (SDP)
   Save up to $10,000 at 10 percent interest in special accounts for troops in a designated war zone.

248. Rest and recuperation (R&R) passes in the most interestingly beautiful places, like Makarska, Croatia; Budapest, Hungary; or Qatar

249. USO—all the comforts of home, away from home
   A lounge chair in a quiet dark room to sleep in, a wake-up call, free coffee and donuts—all while they watch your luggage

   Visit the website at www.uso.org.

250. How focusing on "thirty-nine days and a wake-up" somehow makes it seem shorter than "forty days"

251. Mobile Exchanges

Photo by Kimberly Gearhart

Gary Sinise and the Lt. Dan Band performing at U.S. Army Garrison Schweinfurt, Germany

252. Entertainment tours made possible by USO and Armed Forces Entertainment

A tradition that has continued from WWII to the current wars, USO tours were made most visible by Bob Hope's many Christmas shows, but they also include performances by other greats, from Marilyn Monroe and Bing Crosby to Robin Williams, Kellie Pickler, Toby Keith, and Gary Sinise with the Lt. Dan Band.

> *You are all true examples of what our country was founded on. You are America's courage and you are America's freedom. You are the reason we get to wake up every morning and actually have a choice as to what our individual lives will be like.*
>
> –MODEL-ACTRESS MAYRA VERONICA,
>   speaking to Marines at Camp Lemonier, Djibouti, during a USO visit

253. Other thank-you gestures

★ Being given first-class seating

★ Receiving a standing ovation as you're the first one off a plane

★ Being asked to be a parade marshal for a hometown parade

> *Feeling gratitude and not expressing it*
> *is like wrapping a present and not giving it.*
>
> –WILLIAM ARTHUR WARD

254. Pen pals

> *We still exchange Christmas cards with two*
> *military supportive families, who wrote me—a stranger*
> *to them—while I was deployed to Bosnia in 1999!*
>
> –STAR

255. How deployments to places like Iraq and Afghanistan give you great appreciation for the simplest of daily joys, like the smell of new-cut grass

256. Employer Support of the Guard and Reserve (ESGR)

I took part in coordinating what we called a "Boss Lift" at one Reserve unit. We arranged to bring many of the Reservists' bosses in for one day to observe their employees in training during our two-week annual training. We wanted them to see that what was often called "summer camp" wasn't a vacation time for their employees, since losing them for two weeks was obviously a hardship for each company. Flying the bosses in by helicopter and allowing them to participate in some of the training activities gave them a sense of connection and partnership that helped them be even more supportive of their employees' Reserve duty. We realized from that Boss Lift how powerful this was, especially with employers who formerly had no connection to the military. They left impressed with what they experienced and feeling a new sense of pride of serving in a way by sharing their employee with the military.

–KATHIE

257. "Counting down" rituals that create memories—to the next Permanent Change of Station (PCS), to your return home from duty, to retirement

258. Four-day or ninety-six-hour passes—liberty

259. Training holidays

260. Serving Thanksgiving dinner at the Mess hall/Dining Facility

261. Shore leave

262. PCS orders

263. Military relief societies

Providing emergency financial assistance to Service members via interest-free loans and/or grants
- **Army Emergency Relief** www.aerhq.org
- **Air Force Aid Society** www.afas.org
- **Navy-Marine Corps Relief Society** www.nmcrs.org
- **Coast Guard Mutual Assistance** www.cgmahq.org

264. Thank-you cards or letters from loved ones or supporters back home, collected through various initiatives

INITIATIVES FOR SENDING THANKS

Red Cross and Pitney Bowes
Holiday Mail for Heroes
PO Box 5456
Capitol Heights, MD 20791-5456

Xerox Corporation's Let's Say Thanks
Online postcards
www.LetsSayThanks.com

A Million Thanks
17853 Santiago Blvd. #107-355
Villa Park, CA 92861
Check out the book *A Million Thanks*
by founder Shauna Fleming

Blue Star Families' Operation Appreciation
PO Box 1906
Chesapeake, VA 23327

Photo by Lauren DiCioccio

"Lined paper" machine-sewn by artist Lauren DiCioccio, embroidered by senior citizens, and sent overseas as part of the Blue Star Families', Operation Appreciation

Photo by Skye Piel

265. Welcome-home signs in wire fences made with colored plastic cups—lining the long drive to the installation

266. The Military Channel—"Go behind the lines"

The Military Channel was launched in 1999 by Discovery Communications. Many of its shows are war documentaries, which deal in large part with modern warfare and in particular the U.S. military from World War II. The channel tends to have more contemporary subject matter on wars and conflicts, weapons, vehicles, robots, and snipers than does its competitor the Military History Channel, which tends to show more programs about other periods and forms of warfare (ancient, Roman, Medieval, Eastern, and so on).

Visit the website at www.military.discovery.com.

267. Command Time

268. Advanced leadership training: Command and Staff Colleges, War College, Senior NCO Academies

269. Master Trainers

270. U.S. Navy and Army's Training with Industry fellowships

A program that allows an exchange of best practices and information between various industries and the military

271. Plan of the Day (POD)

272. After Action Reviews (AARs)

273. Command Team Seminars

274. Army and Air Force Exchange Service (AAFES) POGs

"POG" is an acronym for a popular Hawaiian drink made from passion fruit, orange, and guava juices. According to the AAFES Public Affairs Office, the game of POGs originated in the 1920s in Hawaii, when dairy workers played the game during breaks using simple milk caps. Reintroduced in the 1990s, the game has spread.

AAFES adopted POGs as currency in 2001 to support coinage needs for military in the Middle East, where the cost of shipping made metal coins prohibitive. Instead AAFES created these gift certificates worth five, ten, or twenty-five cents. Dubbed POGs, the small discs are thinner and lighter than traditional metal currency and are accepted at Exchanges worldwide.

Sporting distinctive military imagery, POGs have generally been well received and have even become collectors' items. About once a year, AAFES introduces a new POG series, with new designs. Money, a game piece, or a collector's item—What's not to like?

Photo by Dan Rodriguez

★ ★

Commissioning Sources

275. Academies, colleges, and Reserve Officer Training Corps (ROTC)

276. Officer Candidate School (OCS)

277. Direct commission

★ ★

278. Code words and code talkers

279. Sick call

280. "Cup and Flower" fund

281. Military Service magazines that keep us informed
- *Air Force Magazine*
- *Soldiers*
- *GX: The Guard Experience*
- *Warrior-Citizen Magazine*
- *Coast Guard*
- *Futures Magazine: True Stories of Military Service*
- *Leatherneck Magazine*
- *All Hands*

282. Unit T-shirts and other conversation starters like unit jackets and hats, tie tacks, and bumper stickers

283. Boots and Utes!
Uniforms and memories of older uniforms as new ones come into use: from OD green fatigues to BDUs to Desert Storm "chocolate chip" pattern to DCUs (with Elvis colors) to ACUs; from starch to no starch back to starch; from spit-and-shine polish to no polish; from sew-on rank to pin-on rank to Velcro rank.

What are some of your uniform memories and how have uniforms changed since you joined?

Photo by Laura Fleming Photography

284. Dog tags

285. O Club plaque walls

One great example is open to the public at Cubi Bar Café in the National Naval Aviation Museum, Pensacola, Florida. The Museum café is a re-creation of the Officers' Cubi Club previously located in the Republic of the Philippines. From the Vietnam era to the 1990s unit plaques were retired to that Officers Club bar wall. When the original Cubi Club closed, those plaques were brought to the museum in Pensacola for exhibit.

286. Government-issued Blackberries (or rather, "crack" berries)

287. Government-issued credit cards

>>> **DID YOU KNOW?**

If you think your spouse is "the best," you can nominate him or her as Military Spouse of the Year, an award presented by *Military Spouse* magazine.

288. **Being recognized as the best of the best. For example:**
- Airman/Soldier/Sailor/Marine of the Year Award
- Best Ranger Competition
- Prime Power Competition
- International Sniper Competition
- Military Culinary Arts Competition

> *If a man does his best, what else is there?*
> –GEN. GEORGE S. PATTON JR.

289. **Common Access Card (CAC) readers—Out with the old. In with the smart.**
The CAC is a Department of Defense smart card issued as standard identification for active-duty military personnel, Reserve personnel, civilian employees, other non-DoD government employees, state employees of the National Guard, and eligible contractor personnel.

See www.cac.mil.

290. **Memories of "breaking starch"**

291. **Flight suits**

292. **Jump suits**

293. **Name tapes**

294. **Tabs**
- Ranger
- Sapper
- Special Forces

Wear three tabs, known as a "tower of power," and you're known as a "triple threat" with a "triple canopy"!

295. Military prayers or various scripture that military cling to

Praise the Lord and pass the ammunition.
–H.M. FORGY, chaplain, USS *New Orleans*, Pearl Harbor

God is always on the side of the heaviest battalions.
–VOLTAIRE

What do you do to "keep the faith"?

THE SOLDIER'S PSALM

Do not be afraid of the terrors of the night,
nor the arrow that flies in the day.
Do not dread the disease that stalks in darkness,
nor the disaster that strikes at midday.
Though a thousand fall at your side,
though ten thousand are dying around you,
these evils will not touch you.

–Psalms 91:5-7, New Living Translation (NLT)

❧

How beautiful upon the mountains are the feet
of him who brings good news, who proclaims peace …

–Isaiah 52:7a, New King James Version (NKJV™)

❧

There is no greater love than
to lay down one's life for one's friends.

–John 15:13, New Living Translation (NLT)

❧

Also I heard the voice of the Lord, saying:
"Whom shall I send, And who will go for us?"
Then I said, "Here am I! Send me."

–Isaiah 6:8, New King James Version (NKJV™)

296. Airborne school

297. Annual International Lineman's Rodeo, Military Division
Hosted by the International Lineman's Rodeo Association "to provide a forum for the public to better understand and recognize the technical craft skills the linemen have, and to provide an opportunity for the professional craftspeople in the line work trade to receive recognition for their skills"

See www.linemansrodeokc.com.

298. Surplus stores

299. The fun of yelling at the movie screen, "That's not how it happens in the military!" as you view military movies with expert eyes

300. Joint assignments

301. Having the backup of two uniformed noncombatant services
The National Oceanic and Atmospheric Administration (NOAA) and the Public Health Service Commissioned Corps (PHSCC) are classified as noncombatants, unless directed to serve as part of the armed forces by the President or detailed to a Service branch of the armed forces. On a number of occasions in history both the NOAA and PHSCC have been called up for combat missions or national emergencies. As we write this book, there are forty-seven PHSCC officers currently deployed—mostly in Haiti.

> *The Commissioned Corps is the front line of the health of the nation ... As a member of the Commissioned Corps, I feel that I am a weapon against the inequalities that people may face in their medical care.*
>
> –LT. CMDR. NANCY KNIGHT, physician, U.S. Public Health Services

Photo by Pfc. Bailey Jester

Soldiers begin the water jug carries during the "spur ride."

302. Spur rides

Rooted in tradition, spur rides are a rite of passage for members in U.S. Cavalry units. The spur ride involves several tasks that have to be performed as a team, all while hiking with forty to fifty pounds of gear to a number of stations along a difficult course, sometimes lasting days. Soldiers are awarded spurs for their display of initiative, knowledge, and endurance; sometimes combat experience qualifies a Cavalry member as well.

303. Transition assistance from military to civilian, when the time comes
- **Transition Assistance Program (TAP)**
  www.turbotap.org
  Free transition services to Service members and their
  families leaving the military

- **American Corporate Partners (ACP)**
  www.acp-usa.org
  A nationwide mentoring program dedicated to helping
  veterans transition from the armed services to the civilian
  workforce through mentoring, career counseling, and
  networking with professionals from some of America's
  finest corporations and select universities. ACP is not a
  jobs program, but a tool for networking and long-term
  career development. Professionals from ACP's participating
  institutions volunteer to mentor veteran protégés in a
  yearlong mentorship. Those who have served on active duty
  since 2001, as well as the spouses of those Service members
  severely wounded or killed in action, are eligible to apply to
  be protégés, and those with Service-related disabilities will
  be given preference.

- **The Employer Partnership (EP)**
  www.employerpartnership.org
  A way to provide America's employers with a direct link to
  some of America's finest employees—Service members and
  their families. Through the partnership, Service members
  can leverage their military training and experience for
  career opportunities in today's civilian job market with
  national, regional, and local Employer Partners.

- *Military-to-Civilian Career Transition Guide*
  by Janet Farley, JobTalk columnist for *Stars and Stripes*

304. How appreciated and humble you feel when a veteran of a previous war thanks you for your service today

305. Always being the coolest parent visitor on Career Day

Photo by Laura Fleming Photography

306. War-specific books and resources often cathartic in their "shared experiences"

- *Back From War: Finding Hope and Understanding in Life After Combat for the American Soldier & Their Loved Ones* by 1st Lt. Lee Alley with Wade Stevenson
- *Beyond Duty* by Shannon Meehan with Roger Thompson
- *Down Range to Iraq and Back* by Bridget C. Cantrell and Chuck Dean
- *Matterhorn* by Karl Marlantes
- *The Unforgiving Minute* by Craig M. Mullaney
- *We Were Soldiers Once ... And Young* by Harold G. Moore and Joseph L. Galloway

What are your favorite helpful books?

307. Identifying with other Service members

You Know You Are a Service Member When ...

You roll all your clothes before you put them in the dresser

You always back into parking spaces

You don't own any blue ink pens

Your favorite piece of luggage is a duffel bag

All your underwear is colored OD green, brown, or white

You call your hat "a cover"

You call an efficient person "high-speed, low drag" or maybe "lean and mean"

You have to look up your home phone number but can dial the CQ, staff duty, or company numbers without a second thought

The only suit you own is your military-issued dress uniform

You decorate your Christmas tree with chem lights and engineer tape

You answer "squared away" or "shipshape" when someone asks, "How are you?"

You ask someone to hold on a second by saying "stand by"

You refer to your wife as Shipmate, CINC House, or Household 6

You yell "at ease" when your kids are too noisy

You are convinced that coffee is a nutrient

You string concertina wire to keep the neighbor's kids out of your garden

Each page of your vacation atlas has two routes marked

You call the Post Locator instead of Information to find your friends

The only time you and your spouse eat without the kids is at the unit "dining-out"

You answer your phone at home by explaining that the line is unsecure and immediately follow that with "Sir" or "Ma'am"

You make your children clear housing before they go off to college

Your POV is equipped with blackout lights

★

Although you wear no medals
and will reap no glory on the field of battle,
you are a hero in the truest sense of the word.
You are a military spouse.

–JEFF EDWARDS, retired U.S. Navy Chief Petty Officer
and award-winning author

★

ON THE INSIDE

SPOUSE

*You didn't know when you married this wonderful man
that you and your family would be a part of his sacrifice, as well.
You didn't know this military life would be so painful,
so joyful, so difficult—and yet so meaningful.*

–LISA BLACK, Air Force spouse

308. Knowing in your heart that you serve, too

309. The moment of sheer apprehension, fear, excitement, and eagerness when your Service member casually announces your next PCS (Permanent Change of Station)

"We're going WHERE?" Followed by "WHEN?"

310. The way that military spouse life has changed

Gone are the days of hats, white gloves, calling cards, and rules like "only entertain one rank up and two ranks down." Now we have jogging suits, running shoes, e-mail addresses, and teamwork among the ranks.

311. The camaraderie of military spouses

The article on page 86 was written by Debby Giusti and has circulated throughout military posts around the world. She may have been writing about Army wives, but the sentiments and memories apply to all military spouses.

SISTERHOOD

☆

I am an Army Wife—a member of that sisterhood of women who have the courage to watch their men march into battle and the strength to survive until their return. Our sorority knows no rank for we earn our membership with a marriage license, traveling over miles or over nations to begin a new life with our Soldier husbands.

Within days we turn a barren, echoing building into a home, and though our quarters are inevitably white walled and unpapered, we decorate with the treasures of our travels for we shop the markets of the globe.

Using hammer and nail, we tack our pictures to the wall and our roots to the floor as firmly as if we had lived there for a lifetime. We hold a family together by the bootstraps and raise the best of "brats," instilling in them the motto, "Home is Togetherness," whether motel or guesthouse, apartment or duplex.

As Army wives, we soon realize that the only good in "Good-bye" is the "Hello again." For as salesmen for freedom, our husbands are often on the road, leaving us behind for a week, a month, an assignment. During the separation we guard the home front, existing till the homecoming.

Unlike our civilian counterparts, we measure time, not by age, but by tours—married at Knox, a baby born at Bliss, a promotion in Missouri. We plant trees and never see them grow tall, work on projects completed long after our departure, and enhance our community for the betterment of those who come after us. We leave a part of ourselves at every stop.

Through experience we have learned to pack a suitcase, a car, or hold baggage and live indefinitely from the contents within; and though our fingers are sore from the patches we have sewn and the silver we have shined, our hands are always ready to help those around us.

Women of peace, we pray for a world in harmony, for the flag that leads our men into battle will also blanket them in death. Yet we are an optimistic group, thinking of the good and forgetting the bad, cherishing yesterday while anticipating tomorrow.

Never rich by monetary standards, our hearts are overflowing with a wealth of experiences common only to those united by the special tradition of military life. We pass on this legacy to every Army bride, welcoming her with outstretched arms, with love and friendship, from one sister to another, sharing in the bounty of our unique, fulfilling Army way of life.

–©DEBBY GIUSTI, author and Army wife, *www.DebbyGiusti.com*

Photo by Laura Fleming Photography

312. Living an "everyday" life that civilians will never experience

And, oh yes, we call it a base if we are Air Force, Coast Guard, Marine Corps, or Navy. We call it a post if we are Army. Although many things are similar on the installations of the different services, many things are different because of the difference in missions. Here's one example, a day in the life of an Army post:

The day starts at sunrise with the sound of "Reveille" played on a bugle. The exact time varies by post, and the "bugle" these days is usually a recording blasted out from post headquarters as the flag is raised out front.

Reveille is from the French word for "wake up." There are no official lyrics to reveille but many military are familiar with some variation that starts with words like:

I can't get 'em up
I can't get 'em up
I can't get 'em up this morning

If you live on post and aren't personally in the military, you might well wake to the rhythmic sound of feet slapping the pavement outside your house, as a military unit runs by in formation during their morning PT. Post housing is like many housing developments at first glance. However, here they are separated into areas for enlisted, for NCOs, and for officers. The size of the house has traditionally been determined by rank, although as the new privatized housing programs build new homes, the sizes and amenities are changing and improving dramatically for everyone. The generals' homes are still the largest on post and many posts have beautiful historical homes. The officers' homes often circle the parade field. Another difference from civilian life is the fact that each house has a house number but sometimes also a sign with the individual Service member's rank and name.

One big difference from the civilian world is that you won't find anyone much over the age of fifty-five living on post. No retirees here. Early on, most military members lived on post. However, as our military numbers grew that is no longer possible. Many of us live off post these days. Overseas we call that "living on the economy." And oh yes, overseas housing is very different, often apartments rather than houses. Only we call them stairwells rather than apartments for some reason.

A military post is like a complete city in itself, only with different names for key services. We call our department store the "Post Exchange" or "PX," our grocery store the "Commissary," our police station the "MP station," and our liquor store the "Class VI." We used to have snack bars. Now we have fast food restaurants like Burger King, Popeyes, and Starbucks. We have movie theaters, banks, credit unions, post offices, gas stations, fitness centers, churches—which we call chapels no matter the size or denomination—ball parks, schools, and hospitals. Many posts include a golf course; some have horse stables.

It's a self-contained world with access controlled at a front gate. You have to have an official sticker on your car and show your ID card to get through the gate, or else you have to sign in at a visitor's center to get a temporary pass.

Of course, one big difference is that this city within the gates also has landing strips and big training areas that are restricted and often the source of the sound of guns and artillery barrages at all hours, or of jets taking off and landing 24/7.

At the end of the official workday, "Retreat" sounds. Anyone on post who is outside stops at that point, turns towards post headquarters where the flag is, and stands at attention. If you are driving a car on post at that time, you stop the car and get out to stand at attention. When "To the Colors" starts playing as the flag is lowered, you render honors by saluting or putting your hand over your heart. That may be the end of the official duty day, but in many cases, military members continue working long after that.

The last bugle call of the day is "Taps," designating "lights out." That might actually mean "lights out" in the barracks of a basic training company, but certainly not in individual homes. For many military members part of the lyrics to this bugle call are familiar:

Day is done, gone the sun,
From the lake, from the hills, from the sky;
All is well, safely rest, God is nigh.

There are of course many people on duty throughout the night on every military post, from gate guards to staff duty officers and NCOs at post headquarters ready to respond to emergencies and call out units at a moment's notice. Our military world—it really is a 24/7 world.

313. Learning the ins and outs of Czech/German crystal/glass stores from other military spouses

314. Department of Defense (DoD) Priority Placement program for spouses who are Federal government employees

Where did you meet your spouse?

315. For some of us, the military is where we met our spouse and that's one really great thing to love.

316. Losing weight while your spouse is deployed and debuting your new self upon return—what a surprise!

317. The many programs that came about only because a spouse or group of spouses stepped up to advocate for needed change
The first group to get child care going on base, for example, was an enlisted wives association back in 1936.
In 1969, a group of military wives and widows gathered to discuss the fact that, at that time, if you were married to the

military and your spouse died in retirement, his retirement pay stopped. You got nothing despite the many sacrifices you had made. These women formed the National Military Wives Association, which later became the National Military Family Association or simply NMFA. This nonprofit pushed through the Survivor Benefit Plan and has continued to be instrumental in advocating for change. We have them to thank for benefits such as our dental plan, cost-of-living allowance, adoption expense reimbursement, and increased active-duty survivor benefits.

In the 1990s a group of spouses pushed to better prepare military spouses for military life. Army Family Team Building courses resulted and spread to the other services so they all now have "Military 101" type courses to help new spouses learn about this new world they've entered. Spouses helping spouses, for generations to come.

318. "Howitzer" or tank crossing signs

We don't think anything of it after the first time; they're as commonplace to us as deer crossing signs are to civilians.

Photo by Tara Crooks

319. "Battle Buddies"—all in the same boat, fighting the same "battle," making the bonds much easier to form than they are in civilian life

I met my friend and "battle buddy" Cindy at the Hinesville, Georgia, Wal-Mart while standing in line to pick up pictures. She had her son in the cart. I had my daughter. We were both about ready to pull our hair out. When the kids started eyeing each other, we started talking. They played and we learned that she and her husband were from the Midwest as well. She grabbed her pictures and left. I turned to my husband and said, "That's too bad, she seemed normal." He laughed and said, "Who says things like that, Tara?"

I was paying for my pictures when she came back around the corner. She said, "You're going to think I'm strange. Can I get your number? I don't have any friends here and you seem really normal." Kevin just about choked. I laughed and of course explained to her I just said the same thing about her.

To this day, our families are very close. Her second son and my second daughter were born within six months of each other. They have PCS'd overseas and we have flown Space A to visit. It's a bond we know will last a lifetime.

–TARA

Friendship is born at that moment when one person says to another, "What! You too? I thought I was the only one!"
–C.S. LEWIS

Where did you meet your battle buddy?

320. The perfect excuse

"Perfect Excuse Central," an article by Navy spouse Jacey Eckhart in *Military Spouse* magazine, had us laughing and nodding our heads. "Thanks to military life," Eckhart says, "I am always equipped with the perfect excuse for not attending high school reunions—especially when I feel fat. I never have to break up with a girlfriend who doesn't work out. I just move away."

Eckhart goes on to mention also the downside of moving so much, such as missing events like her godchild's First Communion.

We agree wholeheartedly. Yes, it's hard to miss so many important extended family occasions; yes, it's hard as a military spouse to constantly have to start over in our job searches and jobs; yes, it's hard for our spouses to have to adjust to new military bosses so frequently. But just as frequently, your move becomes the perfect excuse or even a blessing.

If it were convenient to gather for every single holiday, we might easily grow tired of it. Kathie has civilian friends who consciously chose to go off by themselves to a motel last Christmas because they couldn't take "another holiday of forced closeness with our extended family," as they described it. Not so for military families. Because of the frequent "excused leaves of absence," the occasional extended-family gatherings are special.

We have all had jobs that we've grown tired of or simply realized were not a good fit. Only we didn't have to get up the nerve to quit. We simply had to say, "So sorry, we have no choice but to leave ... The military is moving us." No need to burn bridges.

Our spouses have all had bosses or co-workers whom they were able to tolerate because they knew the length of time together would be short. Eventually, either the boss was going to PCS or our spouse was.

One of our spouses sees military life as the perfect excuse to avoid extensive "honey-do" yard projects: "I'd love to do that, dear, but we'll be moving in a few short years. We'll do that after retirement."

"Sorry, the military is moving us." Your perfect excuse.

You Know You Are a Military Spouse When ...

All in a week's time, you can pack up a houseful of furniture; pile four kids, two dogs, a cat, three hamsters, a bird, and twelve suitcases into a minivan; drive all the way across country; and still greet your spouse lovingly

Your neighbors know you but have never seen your active-duty spouse

321. Sharing home-front war stories

Once a chaplain (who was a friend) came to my door and told me he was turning me in for "fraud, waste, and abuse." He said, "I know you are trying to get free housing and soak up the benefits of living on a military post." With a straight face he continued, "I know you do not have a husband in the military, because I have never seen him in the two years you have lived here." As I stood there trying to figure out if he was serious or not, the only words that came to me were, "I have e-mails from him to prove I have a husband." HA! That's the only thing that came to mind ... We both laughed and YES he was just kidding. He was just stopping by to check on me.

–HOLLY

322. Dancing on the tables and chairs with hundreds of women at an AWAG conference in Germany

323. Polish pottery trips with friends who know how to get there and where to shop

324. Free access to some of the most amazing fitness centers in the world— and the inspiration of all those fit Service members working out there

325. The fact that your formal military ball gowns/tuxedos can be new again every time you move to a new unit or installation

326. Listening to "jody calls" and the rhythmic running of feet outside your window at "o-dark-thirty"

It's the crack of dawn or "o-dark-thirty," as military members like to say. You hear voices sing out in unison, with one person calling out a line and then the whole unit responding. "Two old ladies lay in bed; one rolled over to the other and said ... I want to be an Airborne Ranger; I want to live a life of danger; Sound off, one ... two ... three ... four, onetwo—threefour." Not only do those "jody calls" help keep everyone in step, they take their minds off the effort of the run.

327. "Fresh starts"

The opportunity for you—and your children—to "reinvent" yourself on a regular basis. From hairstyle to first name!

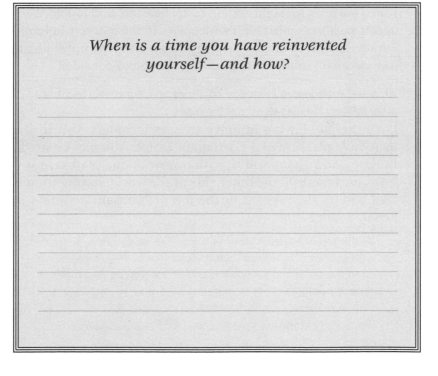

When is a time you have reinvented yourself—and how?

328. Reusing your furniture and changing your décor in each new place

The ancient practice of fêng shui tells you to move twenty-five items to create new energy in a space ... Military spouses do that over and over again.

329. Experiencing cultural delights all over the world

Going to antique markets in Tongeren, Belgium, and Metz, France, while living in Europe. Walking around the traditional Namdaemun and Dongdaemun markets in Seoul, South Korea—a feast for sight, smell, taste, hearing, and touch! Wandering past bags piled high with spices in the markets in Izmir, Turkey, and being invited to have tea in a glass teacup while the rug merchant unfolds rug after rug for you to consider.

330. "Insider" experiences in foreign countries, made possible because other military families show you the ropes

For example, having military friends introduce you to the incredible pleasure of a German or Dutch "therme" or spa in Europe—and giving you tips on proper etiquette to save you from surprises! On the other side of the world, having friends take you on the hike up to the top of Namsan Mountain in Seoul, South Korea.

> At the top of Namsan Mountain, you can do early morning calisthenics with "seasoned" South Koreans who have been doing so to the same music since the end of the Korean War, at which time the exercises were initiated as a way to motivate and inspire war-weary South Koreans.
>
> –CATHY STERLING, Air Force brat, Army wife, advisor and mentor
>   to military families

331. Walking "to Iraq and back" with other spouses and children
A way to be part of the community, get exercise, and feel connected to your spouses who are at war

332. The magic of a Christmas market in Germany

333. Creating new "families" for big holiday gatherings
Single Service members, local friends, and others when you are living far from extended family

334. The sense of satisfaction that comes from preparing "welcome home" kits and programs for single Service members
So they aren't forgotten in the midst of the family reunions as units return from deployment

335. Receiving an eCarePackage from Operation Homefront
Or from anywhere, as long as you didn't have to put it together and take it to the post office—and as long as it's for YOU!

336. Experiencing that sense of continuity
When you discover that your goddaughter (the daughter of another military friend, of course) went to the same Girl Scout camp in Germany—Camp Lachenwald—that you did as a military brat

337. DoD and installation employment resources
- Military Spouse Employment Partnership
- Military Spouse Preference
- Employment Readiness or Assistance programs

338. Meeting your new best friend at an orientation program at your spouse's latest assignment
And still being in close touch twenty-plus years and ten-plus moves later

339. Buying discounted pottery at an Italian outlet
And seeing the same items—priced way above what you paid!—boxed in pallets marked "Nordstrom" as you walk past the checkout

340. The camaraderie and fun of gathering with other spouses or with your children to put together creative care packages for deployed loved ones

Care packages are so much more than what is inside the box. When your loved one is deployed, you have this inherent need to feel connected in some way. Yes, e-mails and Skype and cell phone calls help tremendously. But before those were available and even now that they are, care packages play an important role.

They are called care packages, because you put so much thought into what your husband or wife would most like to receive. You take time to think about them in a different way than you might in day-to-day life. What are their favorite snacks? What are their favorite hobbies? What is not available to them? What must they miss the most about home? What tells them "I love you" or "We miss you"?

Thinking about those things, finding and packing the items, anticipating how they will react when they get and open the box, all connect you or your children to your spouse in a big way.

Often the families of the unit will gather for a potluck and care package evening. Everyone participates to create care packages, long banners that everyone signs and the kids decorate, even video greetings that all the unit members will enjoy.

Of course, once you've sent your first care package, the next time you will wonder, "Okay, now what do I do?" It's a great idea to get inspiration from other spouses.

As we are all so different, the four of us couldn't agree on one favorite care package, so see our favorites on the following pages.

For many more, go to www.ArmyWifeNetwork.com
Click on the EMPOWER tab and in the dropdown
choose CARE PACKAGES.

> Star is good at presenting me with a challenge, and I say, "Don't challenge the master! Care packages are my passion."
>
> –TARA

OUR FOUR FAVORITE CARE PACKAGES

HOW DO YOU EAT YOUR OREOS? CARE PACKAGE

- Original Oreos
- Double Stuf Oreos
- Peanut Butter Oreos
- Mint Oreos
- Golden Oreos
- Chocolate-Covered Oreos
- Low-fat Oreos
- Mini Oreos
- Chocolate Fudge Oreos
- Oreo Cakesters
- Oreo Fun Stix
- Heads or Tails Oreos
- Strawberry Milkshake Crème Oreos
- Oreo 100-Calorie Packs
- Holiday-colored Oreos (blue, yellow, orange, red, or green)
- Oreos ... you get the picture? Lots of Oreos!

MOVIE CARE PACKAGE

- Make a "Now Featuring" movie poster on your computer and add it to the package
- Their all-time favorite movies
- Popcorn (microwave or already popped if they don't have a microwave)
- Movie-size boxed candies
- Caramel popcorn
- Marshmallow rice treats
- Licorice
- Cookies
- Chips & dip
- Nachos

A DAY AT HOME CARE PACKAGE

The idea is to replicate a day with the family. Grab your camera. Take pictures of each thing you do throughout the day, especially those activities that are "ordinary." Use your creativity, but here are a few ideas:

Hi Daddy,

We woke up (take a picture in bed, bed head and all) and ate breakfast (take a picture eating cereal) and then took a shower (take picture in towel). We started the day off by doing some yard work and mowing the lawn (take picture mowing lawn). After our chores we had lunch (take picture with lunch) and then we colored pictures (take pictures doing the activity). We all ate dinner together (take picture having dinner). We had a full day so we were tired when it was time to sit down and watch television (take picture watching television). Later we snuggled up in our pajamas (take picture in pajamas) and had a nighttime snack (take picture snacking). We enjoyed our favorite bedtime story via video (take a picture of the kids listening to the video that your Service member recorded). We love you very much and miss you (take a picture of a goodnight kiss)!

>>> **DID YOU KNOW?**

"Care package" is the most commonly searched-for term on ArmyWifeNetwork.com.

Now, take your pictures and send them with "treats" like these:
- Video of your oldest child reading the same book or just include the book
- Pillowcase sprayed with cologne/perfume or maybe a decorated one
- Several small boxes of his/her favorite cereal or cereal bars
- Shower gel or shampoo or even a soft towel
- Grass clippings in a baggie or dirt from the backyard (strange but reminds them of home)
- Pack a sustainable "brown bag" lunch
- Coloring books and crayons
- DVD of favorite television show
- New pajamas
- Bedtime snack
- Hershey's Kisses

I'M SO BLUE WITHOUT YOU CARE PACKAGE

- Blue corn tortilla chips
- Blue packaged Rice Krispies
- Blue-colored Kool Aid or Gatorade mix
- Blue fleece blanket or new pillowcase
- A blues CD
- Kraft "Blue Box Blues" Easy Mac cups
- Dried blueberries
- Blue-cheese-flavored snacks
- Custom blue M&Ms
- *The Blue Day Book*
- "Blue" movies—For example, *Blue Collar Comedy Hour, The Blues Brothers*, or *Thin Blue Line*

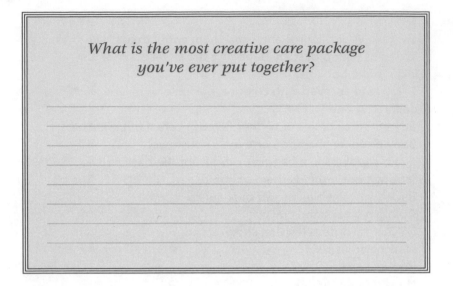

*What is the most creative care package
you've ever put together?*

341. Tiger Cruises

A fun way to let friends and family get a taste of their Sailors'
and Marines' experiences at sea

342. Unit-decorated buckets, pottery, and wood crafts

**343. The scrapbook or piles of handwritten letters, photos, and cards (even
printed e-mails) you saved from separations with your Service member.
One published example is *Dear Diane* by Stephen Bradshaw.**

> *Nothing can replace a handwritten letter. Through those
> beautifully folded pages, he is holding my hand again.*
>
> –MELISSA SELIGMAN, Army wife, author of *The Day after He Left for Iraq*,
> cofounder of HerWarHerVoice.com

**344. The fun of choosing a new activity for you and your spouse or you and
your family to discover and explore at each new assignment**

Kayaking in Washington State, skiing in the Italian Alps, riding
horses in Texas, or waterskiing in Alabama

**345. Helping out at Santa's castle and knowing you make a difference in
children's lives**

346. Being forced to look beyond traditional career paths toward "What can I do here?"

And finding amazing and often unique opportunities to move toward your own dreams as you move from place to place

347. The chance to learn "secrets" of new places from other military spouses

Through shared stories, articles, and books like AWAG's *Never A Dull Moment: Your Guide to Travel in Europe* (13th ed.)

348. Shopping in interesting places

SOME OF OUR FAVORITES

- Itaewon, South Korea
- South Gate (Namdaemun) flea market, South Korea
- Aloha Stadium flea market, Hawaii
- Oriental market in Czech Republic
- Bridge Street in Huntsville, Alabama
- River Street in Savannah, Georgia
- Cayman Islands
- Flea markets in Florence, Italy
- Sommerland in Germany
- Flohmarkt in Bad Dürkheim
- Grand bazaar in Istanbul, Turkey
- Kliczkow castle in Poland
- Thailand's river market
- Fish market in Dieppe, France
- Salzburg, Austria
- Portugal flea markets
- Japanese bazaars
- Open air markets in Russia
- New York City (Chinatown)
- Route 66 in Barstow, California
- Pentagon City mall

Photo by Sgt. Mike Alberts

Spouses of Soldiers assigned to 2nd Squadron, 6th Cavalry Regiment respond to the "Present Arms" command during Spouses' Spur Ride.

349. "GI Jane" Day or being Jane Wayne for a day

350. Claiming the title of "hardest job in the military"

> *You are a patriot—the sort of citizen that all of us should be, but so few of us are. You live with sacrifice, because you believe in the rights and ideals that your [spouse] defends. Although you wear no uniform, you are a part of that defense—a vital link in the chain of freedom. Although you wear no medals and will reap no glory on the field of battle, you are a hero in the truest sense of the word. You are a military spouse.*
>
> –JEFF EDWARDS

351. When a child runs up to anyone in combat boots and uniform (regardless of gender, race, or age) and yells "Daddy!" or "Mommy!"

352. Class VI Package store
   Discounted wine and spirits to celebrate the good moments in life

353. The sense of accomplishment that comes with "holding down the fort" or "keeping the home fires burning"

354. The sound of artillery at 5 a.m.!

355. Jane Wayne Gear, LLC

I am... Strong & Proud, INDEPENDENT, A CREATIVE PROBLEM SOLVER A part of a WORLDWIDE Sisterhood, NOT AFRAID TO CRY, a jet setter, Full of American Pride, A ROCK, Joyous & Thankful, A Cultivator of Patience, IN LOVE WITH A MAN WHO MAKES A DIFFERENCE, Hopeful, a helping hand, WILLING TO LEAN & WANTING TO ♡ BLOOMING WHERE I'VE BEEN PLANTED, SUPPORT, A Friend, Accepting & Forgiving, AN EXPERT IN ACRONYMS, A Believer in almost always, very close to being almost partially in control. QUALITY time, a mover, a shaker, a family motivator, a listener, a shoulder, I am a... a force of nature! MILITARY Wife

Jane Wayne

356. Being able to "read" another military family's house immediately

Walk into many military homes and you can "read" part of the history of their military life. You might find a small wooden house hanging on the wall in the entryway with the saying "Home is Where the Military Sends You." Wooden hearts hang from chains in a line below the house, each heart carved with the name of a military base/post the family has lived on.

Prints by military history artist Don Stivers adorn many military family walls. *The Farewell* is a popular one, showing a Civil War Soldier hugging his wife before heading off to war. It's a reminder that military families have been sacrificing throughout history with separation after separation.

Bookshelves reveal a lot. On one side might be book after book about military history and war, from *The Art of War* by Sun Tzu to Michael Shaara's *The Killer Angels* and *Black Hawk Down* by Mark Bowden. And often W. E. B. Griffin's *The Brotherhood of War*. On the other side of the shelf you might find books about military life from the home-front side: *The Homefront Club* by Jacey Eckhart; *Separated by Duty, United by Love* by Shellie Vandevoorde; Melissa Seligman's *The Day after He Left for Iraq*.

Many military members proudly display military coin collections, either in wooden stands on a desk or in glass-covered display wall boxes. Walk into a home office or den and you likely will find an "I Love Me" wall, displaying all the plaques and awards from units and schools during a military career.

Rugs from Afghanistan or Turkey could indicate assignments in those countries or be reminders of temporary duty trips or deployments. If assignments have led to Okinawa, Japan, or Hawaii, the house may have more Asian-influenced art and furniture.

Other homes may show a European influence, with Belgian tapestry pillowcases and German table linens. Coast Guard families might have Native American art from Alaska or beach art from Cape Cod or Florida. No matter where the military assignments took the military member and their family, their homes tell their stories. They can be fun to "read."

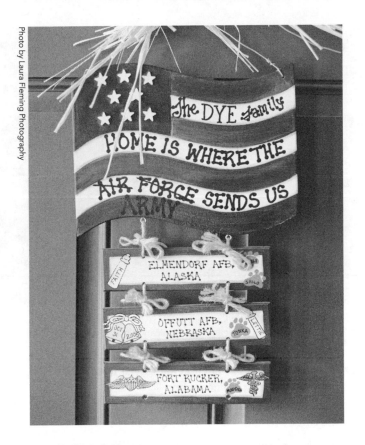

Photo by Laura Fleming Photography

357. Yahoo IM conversations with your Service member at 2 a.m. Ding!

358. Help with the "military spouse" job search
- **Military Spouse Corporate Career Network (MSCCN)**
  www.msccn.org
- **Military Spouse Career Center (MSCC)**
  www.military.com/spouse

359. The excitement of finding that curtains from the old house fit the windows of the new one

360. Your family *not* visiting during your husband or wife's two weeks of R&R

Lt. Col. Nathan Blood, 4th Brigade Combat Team, 10th Mountain Division (Light), and daughter, Mackenzie, during a webcam communication

361. Explaining to your two-year-old that Mommy or Daddy (who is deployed) doesn't live in the computer

Or explaining that they can't "just come home" from TDY, a school, or deployment to "spend the night"

> *It takes a very special person to be a military spouse.*
> *Their husbands or wives take an oath and sign a contract*
> *when they join the Army. Military spouses are enlisted*
> *the day they take their wedding vows. As a husband*
> *to my wonderful wife, Sarah, I want to say thank you*
> *to all the military spouses. Your love, support, and sacrifice*
> *are an inspiration and keep us Army strong.*
>
> –LT. GEN. RICK LYNCH, U.S. Army

362. How the view of spouses has changed over time:

★ **Early Army view:** "If the Army wanted you to have a wife, they would have issued you one."

★ **Early Navy view:** "Navy wives were not issued in sea bags."

363. When someone asks you why or how do you do it

Military spouses who have been around for a while represent a small group and have a unique expertise. It would be selfish to not share or reach out to others who are experiencing some of the same issues and concerns. I know that everyone handles these types of things differently, but I do my best to advocate resiliency. I have said to myself regarding my husband's deployments, "He has his mission, and I have mine." I believe if the family is able to cope, the Soldier is able to stay battle-focused and safe, not having that constant worry about home and their loved ones.

–JULIE SHIBUSAWA, Army veteran, Army wife, and Army mom

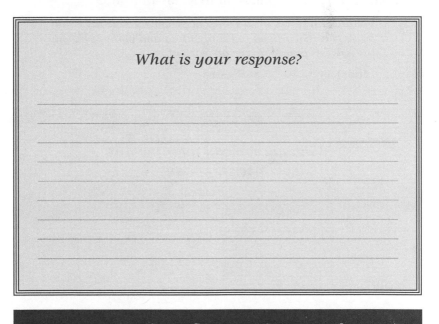

What is your response?

You Know You Are a Military Spouse When ...

People say, "I don't know how you handle the military lifestyle," and you say, "I couldn't imagine my life any other way"

364. The level to which military spouses step up and volunteer

According to the Blue Star Families' Military Family Lifestyle Survey 2010 (3,634 military families surveyed), 68 percent of respondents had volunteered in the last year. A direct comparison with civilian volunteers isn't possible given the difference in definitions and populations, but the Corporation for National and Community Service indicated that in 2009 the national volunteer rate was just under 27 percent.

The majority of military-affiliated volunteers carve out less than ten hours a month in any one category of donated time (to military non-profits or church, for example). However, 9 percent of the respondents who declared hours put in more than thirty hours per month—equivalent to a part-time job.

Volunteering gives me a group of people outside my home and my neighborhood to fill my mind and perhaps become my newest "family" in the absence of my own.

–THERESA DONAHOE, Army spouse

What are some of your favorite volunteer experiences?

365. Spouse clubs

★ Bunco parties

★ Luncheons

★ Wild West night, aka Denim and Diamonds or Monte Carlo night

★ Bazaars or craft fairs—Whether CONUS (continental United States) or OCONUS (outside the continental United States), bazaars are places where you can get your entire family gift-buying done in one place. Not to mention, add a few things to your home décor too.

★ Tours—The club takes care of all the arrangements. Visit Florence, Italy, from Germany, or New York City from D.C. to see the Rockettes at Christmastime.

366. Volunteer awards

There are many local and Service-branch–oriented volunteer awards out there; here are a few from the national level:

- **National Military Family Association (NMFA) Family Award**—Highlights the public service of military families who serve their nation. Recipients receive a cash award and are flown to Washington, D.C., where they are honored.
- **National Military Family Association Very Important Patriot Award**—Recognizes exceptional volunteers whose outstanding service contributes to improving the quality of life in their military and/or local civilian communities.
- **"Newman's Own" Award for Excellent Military Community Service**—Awards grants to private organizations whose innovative program improves the quality of life for military families and their communities.
- **AUSA Rubbermaid Volunteer Family of the Year Award**

367. The memory of spit-shined boots, which really did mean "spit"

Or that bit of water and ice trick. Especially fun to see your macho spouse using pantyhose—of all things—to buff that shine.

You Know You Are a Military Spouse When ...

Your husband just left for TDY and the radiator blows up on the car and the washing machine dies

368. "Semper Gumby"—the battle cry of the military spouse

When Sarah Selvidge, an Army spouse, was living overseas and her husband was deployed for ten months, her car engine gave out. She found a Soldier mechanic who was willing to fix her car if she could get another engine. Amazingly, the next thing she knew she was on her way to the junkyard to "pluck an engine" out of another car. It was something she had never done before in her life, but knew she had to do in order to have transportation. Not only did she "pluck" that engine but she even assisted the mechanic in getting the car running again.

I am military spouse—hear me roar!

369. Some of the hardest things about moving: the hunt for a hairstylist/barber, a dentist, and a groomer/veterinarian for your pets

What is the hardest part of moving for you?

370. Knowing that no matter where you are on your journey someone is right there with you who shares the experience or can mentor you because they've "been there and done that"

Coasties and their families are the most supportive people I've met. Our wedding reception was also our going-away party, as we were moving from Washington, D.C., to Homer, Alaska, two days later. I will always be grateful for all the Coast Guard wives who were there who rushed me at the reception to tell me about all the adventures I had ahead of me. I had never met them (my husband worked with their husbands), but they made a point to share words of wisdom for the journey ahead of me. This was such a breath of fresh air after all the fears and concerns about military life expressed by well-meaning civilians in my life.

–JOCELYN GREEN, author of *Faith Deployed: Daily Encouragement for Military Wives*

What is a great experience someone shared with you?

371. Male military spouses and their unique perspective

When it comes to the term "military spouse," there's an immediate assumption that you're talking about women. You'd be hard-pressed to find support services catering to military husbands compared with those that support military wives. That's because only 6 to 8 percent of military spouses are male and of that relatively small number, fully 60 to 80 percent are former military themselves. It's hard to make the connection and to get male spouses as involved as female spouses.

The good news is that our military is starting to recognize the growing percentage of military spouses who are men. They're slowly but surely creating programs that cater to the population, as they realize this population has unique views and concerns that affect military families.

Women are creatures of togetherness. They like to take journeys in groups for emotional support. Give a woman a map and she will ask her friends for interpretation and experience with the trip. They want solutions, but it might take a lengthy discussion to get to the perfect one. Some women may go on a journey just because their friend wanted them to go along.

Men like maps, but they don't like to ask for directions. They need to know how to go from point A to point B and arrive at the destination competently. They want solutions to fix the problem. You will have to give a man a reason for why he needs to take the trip.

These and other differences are what many military programs are trying to figure out how to navigate. Because both sides of the coin are helpful in different situations, you have to love that all military spouses, especially the minority, are finding their voices.

> *It is an honor and a privilege as a military spouse to stand behind and beside our spouse, but as a male military spouse—what I call a ManSpouse—the challenge is extremely tough. Like our female military spouse counterparts we need a network to lean on, but we are not like women—we don't bond by just being together, we bond by doing together.*
>
> –WAYNE PERRY, *TheArmyWife(DUDE)* blog

Photo by Whitney Beasley

A collage of stickers from a Coast Guard family's many moves

372. Finding moving stickers of different colors on your furniture years after retiring from the military

373. Watching your spouse so carefully roll their uniform pants leg around those blousing bands

374. Volunteering to work at an installation thrift shop and getting "first dibs" on items that come in

375. Lunch outside in the inner courtyard of the Pentagon

376. The laugh you get when you take the clothes out of the dryer and have to pry your unmentionables off the Velcro on your Service member's uniform

377. Volunteer Management Information System (VMIS) at MyArmyOneSource.com

378. Military spouses who have written books to help others learn how to navigate this military life without having to learn things the hard way

We couldn't begin to list them all; here are some favorites:

- *A Family's Guide to the Military for Dummies* by Sheryl Garrett and Sue Hoppin
- *Faith Deployed … Again!* by Jocelyn Green
- *Help! I'm a Military Spouse—I Get a Life Too!* by Kathie Hightower and Holly Scherer
- *Heroes at Home* by Ellie Kay
- *Household Baggage Handlers* by Marna Krajeski
- *I'm Already Home … Again!* by Elaine Dumler
- *National Guard 101: A Handbook for Spouses* by Mary Corbett
- *Separated by Duty, United by Love* by Shellie Vandevoorde
- *That Military House* by Sandee Payne
- *The Homefront Club* by Jacey Eckhart

What are your favorite military spouse books?

379. Military Wife recipe

Get your own handcrafted solid pine "Recipe for a Military Wife" sign at OldGlorySoldiers.com.

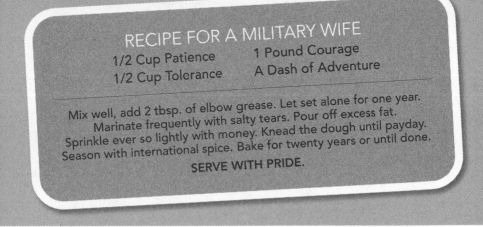

RECIPE FOR A MILITARY WIFE

1/2 Cup Patience   1 Pound Courage
1/2 Cup Tolerance   A Dash of Adventure

Mix well, add 2 tbsp. of elbow grease. Let set alone for one year.
Marinate frequently with salty tears. Pour off excess fat.
Sprinkle ever so lightly with money. Knead the dough until payday.
Season with international spice. Bake for twenty years or until done.
SERVE WITH PRIDE.

380. Protestant Women of the Chapel (PWOC)

A network that unites, trains, and encourages women in the military chapel community in their spiritual growth

381. Military Council of Catholic Women (MCCW)

A visible presence of Christ in military communities

382. Being able to proudly call yourself "Household 6" or "Commander in Chief" (CINC) of the house!

383. Household appliances that seem to know when deployments happen

It doesn't even have to be an appliance. During my husband's second deployment, the whole house fell down around me. No kidding! Cabinets—the ones the builders put in—literally fell off the wall into a crashing pile of dishes on my floor. I just stood there and laughed. What else could I do? You can't make this stuff up.

–TARA

384. "First Kiss" over and over

Military wives live lives full of passion. The good-byes with teary, long kisses; homecomings that make your heart skip a beat just like you were dating again; the first kiss after a deployment; having your heart ache with loneliness; getting really angry when something breaks and your man isn't around to fix it ... Strong emotions make you feel more alive than most people ever feel when they get into a marriage rut.

–MELINDA SHAHA, retired blogger, *Loving A Soldier* blog

Photo by Stephanie Himel-Nelson

Describe one of your "first kisses"

_____
_____
_____
_____
_____
_____
_____
_____
_____
_____
_____
_____
_____
_____
_____
_____
_____
_____
_____
_____

385. Having a baby or raising a child at the same time/age as many other military spouses

Either a "deployment surprise" nine months down the road from a reunion or a "birthday baby" nine months after the Marine Corps birthday or military ball

386. **Military spouse bloggers who share their experiences and help other military families**

We couldn't begin to list them all; here are some favorites:

- *Army Dad* www.armyspouseami.blogspot.com
- *Christian Military Wives Ministry* www.WivesinBloom.com
- *Family Matters* www.afps.dodlive.mil
- *Her War, Her Voice!* www.herwarhervoice.com
- *Homefront in Focus* www.homefrontinfocus.com
- *Household 6 Diva* www.household6diva.com
- *Loving A Soldier* www.lovingasoldier.com
- *Our Hope Endures* www.katieandbenupdates.blogspot.com
- *Spouse Buzz* www.spousebuzz.com
- *Spouse Calls* www.stripes.com/spouse-calls-blog

What are your favorite blogs?

387. Military spouse T-shirts

My husband/wife serves so yours won't get drafted

Don't confuse your rank with my authority

Military Spouse: sexually deprived for your freedom

388. Knowing your spouse's "last four" without hesitation—and yes, having to look up your own

389. MyCAA (Career Advancement Account)—potential free money for a military spouse's education

390. First Steps program—greeting you and your new baby with a welcome basket and information

Free support and counseling following the birth of your baby

391. Military spouse conferences

Military spouses have always reached out to help other military spouses adjust to the challenges of this military life, often one-on-one, but also by creating conferences. The AWAG (Americans Working Around the Globe, formerly American Women's Activities in Germany) conference in Germany might be the oldest—they celebrated their fifty-sixth anniversary in May 2011!

Army wives Judi Bramlett and Sharon Gilliam might be credited as the "Mothers of Military Spouse Conferences in the United States" since their 1988 conference called "Army Wife: A Woman for All Seasons" in Hawaii drew 300 wives to network and learn. As Bramlett says, "In those days, the Army didn't have any classes for spouses whose husbands were not in leadership positions, so this conference was the beginning of training for spouses."

Now the Services all have "Military 101" type programs for spouses, from Army Family Team Building and Marine Corps L.I.N.K.S. to the Navy's COMPASS and Air Force's Heart Links. However, the conference format is still valuable. When else do you get from 100 to 450 military spouses in one building to learn from one another?

Bramlett went on to start a conference in Alaska and later helped design a conference in Hawaii for wives of all Services known today as the Joint Spouses' Conference. Gilliam started a spouse conference at Fort Lewis, Washington, in 1995.

Marine spouses started a conference years ago in El Toro, California. When El Toro closed, spouses took the program to Camp Pendleton. It's evolved and continues today as the Leadership Education Seminar.

In 2007, Tara Crooks and Star Henderson of Army Wife Network hit the conference circuit creating a spouse conference titled Field Exercise. Field Exercise events are a grassroots effort to empower and rejuvenate military spouses nationwide. The pair works closely with installation departments of Family Morale, Welfare, & Recreation, which allows seminars to be held on location. The hundreds of spouses who attend enjoy a time of networking, camaraderie, support, and resources.

Many military communities—and often the family directorates at higher headquarters such as HQ U.S. Marine Corps and HQ U.S. Army Europe—coordinate events for spouses. These workshops, often including the half-day Follow Your Dreams While You Follow the Military workshops with Holly Scherer and Kathie Hightower, have been held across the United States and in Europe, South Korea, and Japan. The Military Officers Association of America just sponsored their fifth annual Military Spouse Symposium in May 2011 with the theme "Keeping a Career on the Move."

If you see an announcement for a military spouse conference or workshop, run and sign up. These don't come around every day. Tap into the wealth of knowledge and networking available. One thing is certain: You'll be uplifted, enlightened, motivated, and strengthened in your life as a military spouse.

392. Military spouse business support

- **Military Spouse Business Association (MSBA)**
  www.milspousebiz.org
  Founded by military spouse entrepreneurs for military spouse entrepreneurs, MSBA membership is free to all active-duty military spouses. In addition to pertinent articles, the Facebook page provides a dynamic area where members can ask questions, share their experiences, and discuss the unique challenges that military spouses face while running their own businesses.
- **National Military Spouse Network (NMSN)**
  www.nationalmilitaryspousenetwork.com
  The preeminent networking, mentoring, and professional development organization committed to the education, empowerment, and advancement of military spouses.
- **Military Spouse Foundation**
  www.militaryspousefoundation.org
  The Military Spouse Foundation is focused on supporting portable career and business development opportunities through educational programs and scholarships. These programs are designed and supported by military spouse professionals.

393. Army Wife Network at www.armywifenetwork.com

Army Wife Talk Radio was born on a whim, during my husband's first deployment. I had created my blog *Loving A Soldier*. The responses I received from my blog helped me realize my own experiences and need for resources formed a common thread with other military spouses. Because of my frequent stints on "Work at Home Mom" talk radio for one of my earlier businesses, I was familiar with Internet "radio." The host kept saying to me, "You should have your own show." I decided to do just that.

–TARA

That's how the original talk radio show "for Army wives, by Army wives" began. Soon, what started out as a fun "hobby" in April 2005 grew in popularity and took on a life of its own.

Through the years it has changed from thirty minutes to up to two hours, and currently is a ninety-minute weekly broadcast featuring up-to-date information, tips and empowerment, and live chat. All the shows are archived as well for spouses to listen to while "on the go," catering to the mobile lifestyle.

INTERACTIVE EMPOWERMENT FOR ARMY WIVES

I happened upon AWTR late one night when my husband was deployed and I was looking for help. It was "off-post, anytime, anywhere help," which I appreciated. I was excited to find someone who had similar struggles and interests, so much so that I wanted to help Tara help other wives.

–STAR

In April 2009, Army Wife Network (AWN) became the umbrella that joined Army Wife Talk Radio (AWTR) and Field Problems (FP).

The mission? To empower those who follow by providing relevant resources and information, networking opportunities (in person and online), and expert advice. AWN holds true to its tagline "Interactive Empowerment for Army Wives" and is now a bustling community of military families sharing information and resources, with more than thirty thousand members and growing.

394. Power of Attorney (POA)

395. Flat-rate shipping boxes for APO and FPO

The sign at the post office catches my attention, of course. When you are writing a book called *1,001 Things to Love about Military Life*, seeing the words GI and Love together jumps out at you. "GI Love Flat Rate Boxes. 900,000 military packages sent." That's a lot of love flying back and forth across the world.

–KATHIE

396. Military Spouse Residency Relief Act

The relief of not having to change your driver's license every time you move to a new state

397. Having friends who understand when you say, "I'm thrilled that he/she's home safe, but he/she's driving me crazy."

398. Port visits where you can fly over and meet the ship—especially fun when a group of spouses go together.

I was only married for about two months before leaving on my first deployment. Because of the work-up schedule, my bride and I weren't able to go on a honeymoon. So when I heard we might have a port visit during the deployment, I was very excited at having the opportunity of a port visit/honeymoon with my wife. With the prospect of Venice as the port, we felt it would be perfect. I had only been in my squadron for a very short amount of time and was worried that I was going to have to be on watch the entire time, but the Junior Officers pulled together and worked out the watch schedule so that we could all get off the boat at some point. My wife, who was also in the Navy at the time, flew into Venice with a few of the other spouses from the squadron. Because port visits are always changing, everyone knew the risk that it might not work out. But we were lucky. We got to spend a full four days and nights together in Venice and it was amazing. We saw the canals, toured the stores, and fed the birds on the Piazza San Marco. Not too shabby for a makeshift honeymoon.

–LT. CMDR. MIKE GREENTREE, U.S. Navy, Naval Flight Officer

Mike and I were married on the weekend I graduated from Supply Corps School. We were both immediately checking into our first commands. We actually had to drive to Virginia the day after we got married because Mike could only get a few days' leave. I joked that our "honeymoon" was the car drive up together. After spending our first married Christmas with me on duty on the ship and with him deployed, it was awesome to hear that there might be a chance of a port visit—to Venice no less! It was very iffy, but a group of us spouses decided to go for it. If the guys didn't end up getting to pull in, we would have a holiday in Venice without them. We all were excited when we heard the Admiral's wife was going—that was "the sign" it was going to happen. I remember the whole thing was so exciting—travelling with the group, seeing Mike for the first time as we pulled up on one of the water taxis, experiencing a new culture with him, and sharing it all with our friends from the squadron. He bought me

Photo by Stephanie Himel-Nelson

a cameo broach and an antique lace tablecloth. We also bought two beautiful charcoal drawings from a wonderful artist who had a display on a street corner and they hang in our guest room today. They always remind me of our "Navy" honeymoon. It wasn't what I had planned for, but it was everything I'd ever dreamed of.

–VIVIAN GREENTREE, Navy veteran and spouse,
   Director of Research and Policy for Blue Star Families

399. The experience of helping, mentoring, or empowering another military spouse

400. Parking spaces for expectant mothers and spouses of deployed members at the Exchange and Commissary
How that shows the change in our military world—acknowledging the spouse and family! In years past, the only reserved spaces were "Any General Officer" or reserved spaces at unit buildings marked "CO" or "CSM."

401. The many states that provide free college tuition to military spouses or in-state tuition for spouses and families

402. Advanced training for military spouses beyond the Military 101 courses:
- Facilitating, Leadership, and Group Skills (FLAGS) program for senior spouses
- The Joint Senior Spouse Course
- Enlisted Spouse Training Series

403. "Murphy's Law"

The only thing you can expect as a military spouse is the unexpected, and if it's going to happen, it's going to happen during a deployment.

404. Spouse coffees

SPOUSE COFFEES, NOT JUST FOR COFFEE

- **Movie night**—Flavored popcorn, nachos, soft pretzels, movie theater candy, and movie trivia quiz. Watch a movie and have door prizes that are movie related.
- **Coffee by committee**—For those who hate to cook. Have everyone bring something to make a salad or sandwich bar. Also have them bring their own topping for a potato or ice cream bar.
- **Soap opera night**—Come all dolled up and everyone gets a soap opera name. You take your middle name as your first and the street you grew up on as your last. If your street is a number, choose your subdivision or town.
- **Scavenger hunt**—Create an installation-wide hunt, a purse hunt, or one around the location of the coffee.
- **Wine and cheese**—Have everyone bring their favorite wine or cheese dish to share.
- **Get resourceful**—Have everyone bring a local resource to share and one local resource they are searching for and go around the room one person at a time. You'll learn so much and it makes it easy to "make conversation" even for the shy guests.

405. The Announcer Guy—you know ... the one who stands between you and your spouse during redeployment

Okay, let me begin by letting my dear friends out there who have been privileged enough to listen to the announcer guy from the bleachers [know] ... I AM TRULY HAPPY FOR YOU! However, ... I am tired! Tired of hearing the Fort Stewart announcer guy say, "Are you ready to wake up, Fort Stewart?" or "They will take even longer if you don't yell louder"... Sometimes he says, "Are you ready to welcome these Soldiers home?"... All to which a very excited crowd responds happily and with a ton of gusto!

Yesterday at the PX, we saw a car that had writing all over it when my three-year-old (who cannot even read) spunkily announced, "There's a daddy home! Is my daddy coming home now?"... This morning my ten-year-old came and curled up in my bed and announced, to my dismay, the torture of living here so close to all of the happy shouts. I did my best to happily explain to her how excited she should be for her friends and all the families that are getting their mommies and daddies back ... Imagine my happy face explaining as I am trying my best to hold my tears at bay ... Don't get me wrong, I love this life and so do my three little ladies ... but that announcer guy makes it pretty hard sometimes.

[But as] I sat silently this morning just kinda venting to God ... I thought about the legacy of Welcome Home ceremonies that have taken place on Cottrell Field. I am honored to listen to them because, if nothing else, they symbolize freedom to me. Not many people in the U.S., let alone the world, will ever get to experience those sounds—joy in the very purest sense of the word.

So, I will continue to be happy for you guys who are in your moments of complete peace and exhilaration. For one day, I know it will be our turn to get all glammed up and sit on those bleachers awaiting our handsome Soldier to squeeze the life out of us. However, right now, I still want to go and knock the announcer guy out. I won't (probably), but I'll want to just the same.

–NIKKI ACKLES, contributor, *Loving A Soldier* blog

406. The Deployment Cycle

The Department of Defense has an amazingly descriptive deployment cycle written by psychologists that is very technical. This is the deployment cycle written from a military spouse perspective:

Predeployment: Freaking out over the thought that you will be spending more than thirty days without your spouse, feeling like you can't go on, irritated that you have to fill out paperwork and have someone tell you "You're going to make it" because you don't care about even thinking about it happening. It's not fair, you don't like it, and you're in denial that your Soldier is actually leaving.

Deployment: HOLY CRAP, he left. How did that happen? You're not going to make it. How will you ever survive? You will come home from the "drop-off" to his laundry, coffee cup from breakfast, and socks still lying on the floor. You won't move these things for weeks. Day one will be the first day followed by three more days of crying and locking yourself in your bedroom with a box of Oreos, a glass of milk, stash of tissues, his T-shirt, sappy movies, in your pajamas. Your life is on hold— you sleep with the phone next to your ear and the Domino's man knows your order by heart. Day four, he calls and you wake up and realize you haven't brushed your teeth in four days. You need to get it together.

Sustainment: You got it together. Whew! You're on a schedule. You found a battle buddy. You can do this. You will do this. You clean up the house and put all his stuff away in its place. You are taking care of the house, the car, the kids—who has time to realize you're lonely? You start functioning like a well-oiled machine. Well, for the most part. There are moments of intense "I AM SO ALONE" feelings—like when confronted with a friend whose spouse is home, or a sad song on the radio, or when you miss the one time he gets to call that week. That's usually about the same time that the washer breaks and floods your floor or one of the kids breaks a leg. But you're strong and you know this and you start counting down the days to R&R leave.

R&R: Now this really needs its own "pre," "during," and "post," don't you think? Pre: freaking out over him coming home, figuring out how you're going to get in an appointment for your highlights and waxing between going to the grocery store to find all of his favorite things, cleaning the house, and worrying if he is going to love you the same way as when he left. During: read as "HONEYMOON" or "HELL," really depending on the situation and circumstances. Post: repeat Deployment.

Redeployment: Somewhere between pre-R&R and "OH THANK GOD." You're thanking your lucky stars he is coming back to you unharmed. You're worried about how he'll transition. Will you have to deal with effects of his deployment? If so, how? What? This time is usually coupled with several vacation or leave plans, an impending PCS, and/or retirement—just to keep you on your toes! Nothing fazes you though; you have your Soldier home. Happy, Happy, Joy!

Postdeployment: Ahhh, this is about three months later, about the same time you realize that for the last month you have given up your "me" time. You developed a schedule during deployment that has been smashed to smithereens and you haven't watched *The Bachelor* or *Grey's Anatomy* in weeks. Your children aren't sure which one of their parents to listen to and have figured out how to pit you against each other. You have spent WAY too much time with your relatives lately. The impending PCS is getting on your nerves and stressing you out. Then you stop and think about how lucky you are to wrap your arms around your spouse tonight. You smile when you see your children climbing all over their daddy. You have a complete family at the dinner table at night. You get to go out on dates. You have someone to help hold and entertain the children. And at 5 p.m. (OK, realistically? 7 or 8), you can actually expect to see someone walk in the door. You realize that "me" time is worth the trade, and also that this is why God gave us DVRs.

–TARA

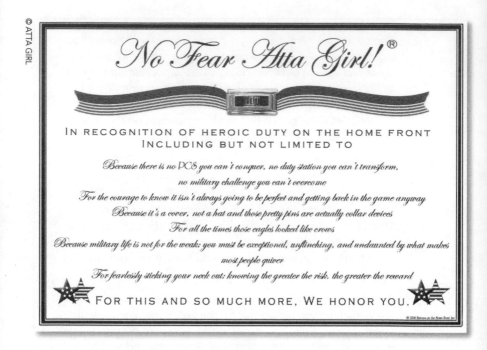

No Fear Atta Girl!®

IN RECOGNITION OF HEROIC DUTY ON THE HOME FRONT
INCLUDING BUT NOT LIMITED TO

Because there is no PCS you can't conquer, no duty station you can't transform,
no military challenge you can't overcome
For the courage to know it isn't always going to be perfect and getting back in the game anyway
Because it's a cover, not a hat and those pretty pins are actually collar devices
For all the times those eagles looked like crows
Because military life is not for the weak: you must be exceptional, unflinching, and undaunted by what makes
most people quiver
For fearlessly sticking your neck out: knowing the greater the risk, the greater the reward

FOR THIS AND SO MUCH MORE, WE HONOR YOU.

407. Atta Girl! Gifts at www.attagirlgifts.com

Home of the original military spouse and military family ribbon awards, Atta Girl! awards honor our home-front heroes for their military life achievements.

> *I got Danielle a bracelet from Atta Girl! and she loved it. Thank you for that advice. I also gave the link to a friend of mine, and his wife was very happy as well. Just thought you should know, you were responsible for making at least two women cry.*
>
> –GUNNERY SGT. SHANE GREEN, U.S. Marine Corps

408. Confessions during deployments

Or at least, a few of the things we're willing to put on paper: eating cereal/popcorn for dinner, living in sweats, going unshaven for longer than should be allowable

409. Command sponsorship

410. Identifying with other military spouses

411. Military Spouse Prayer

Lord, grant me the greatness of heart to see,
the difference in duty and his love for me.
Give me the understanding to know,
that when duty calls he must go.
Give me a task to do each day,
to fill the time when he is away,
And Lord, when duty is in the field,
please protect him and be his shield.

–AUTHOR UNKNOWN

You Know You Are a Military Spouse When ...

You start to tell the movers the correct way to pack moving boxes

Your heart races when you hear the doorbell ring during a deployment

You just spent your second wedding anniversary in a row alone

You have eight different address changes in nine years, and you are not running from the law

If you have a power of attorney, you USE IT, and freak out when it expires

You know all of your spouse's co-workers by their last name and rarely know their first name or even sex

You write only in pencil because EVERYTHING is subject to change

You have enough camouflage in your house to wallpaper the White House

You don't bat an eyelash at 2245 and 0300 duty times

Military homecomings on TV bring tears to your eyes because you can relate so well

You check your e-mail multiple times an hour in hopes that your spouse has e-mailed you, and you know how horrible e-mail being "down" is

You wouldn't dream of going anywhere without your cell phone and all your other numbers forwarded to it

You can hold down the fort while your spouse is deployed or in the field

You know better than to shop the Commissary on the first or fifteenth day of the month

You've slept with a laptop

You refer to everyone not in the military, married to the military, or dating someone in the military as a civilian

You constantly have to explain to businesses on the phone that your spouse can't call to fix the problem because he/she is in the middle of a desert somewhere

You yell at your kids by saying, "Don't make me e-mail your father/mother!"

You say 1800 hours instead of 6 p.m.

Every morning before breakfast you holler at the kids "Fall in!"

You have ever given your spouse or children a counseling statement for not doing the dishes or taking out the trash

You give your kids a hand receipt when they take your Tupperware to school

You refer to your vacation time as "leave"

You aren't surprised when you get four days' notice for a four-month deployment

You have a large collection of different size and color window treatments

You remember milestones by duty stations

You reach for your ID card upon entering a civilian store

You can put nine rooms of furniture in a six-room apartment

You own several military cookbooks published by family support groups

Photo by Michelle Mims, Silhouettes by Michelle

★

I am the person I am today because of
all the places I've lived as a military brat and spouse,
and because of all the people I've met along the way!
I can't imagine a better life!

–CATHY STERLING,
Air Force brat, Army wife, advisor
and mentor to military families

★

ON THE INSIDE

FAMILY

We believe while the road is tough, it is traversable,
and the journey of a military family has inherent value measured
in enriched life experiences, pride, and sense of honor.

–TARA CROOKS AND STARLETT HENDERSON

412. Old Glory

As you stand before the American flag, there is nothing like knowing the meaning of our life is wrapped up right there in red, white, and blue.

Many a bum show has been saved by the flag.

–GEORGE M. COHAN, composer of "You're a Grand Old Flag"

413. Staying connected to friends across the globe virtually by e-mails, Skype, and websites

414. The tears that start when a perfect stranger stops you to say, "Thanks for your service" or "Thanks for your family's sacrifice"

415. Choosing your family

Most of us know the quote as "You can choose your friends but you can't choose your family"—but in the military your friends are your family!

416. Being welcomed to the community with cookies or cake on a plate and the fun of welcoming the new families

The Green Plate Story

Shortly after settling into a new home in Fort Leavenworth, Kansas, I filled a simple green plastic plate with cookies and took them next door to make new friends, Tammy and Dwayne Williams. The friendship between the two families grew as the green plate was passed back and forth, always filled with baked goods.

Within ten months, it was time for both families to move again. We were assigned to Colorado, and the Williams family were assigned to Washington, D.C. As we were packing up, Tammy Williams returned the same green plate, saying it was a symbol and a reminder of our friendship.

Three months later on September 11, 2001, Maj. Dwayne Williams was killed at the Pentagon. At that moment the simple green plastic plate took on a whole new meaning. It became a visual reminder of how precious our time on Earth really is.

I wrote the book *The Green Plate* as a tribute to Maj. Dwayne Williams and as a reminder to all of us about the wonderful opportunities we are afforded, as military families, to meet new people, experience new places, and make a difference!

I knew I was only going to be in Fort Leavenworth for ten months, but I'm so glad I got to know that wonderful family and spent time with them.

As soon as *The Green Plate* was released, the book was used by the V Corps Special Troops Battalion as its tool to welcome new families to the unit. Each month, on "Green Plate Day," spouses baked sweets to put on green plastic plates, added information about the unit, and included *The Green Plate* story. These were delivered to the spouses of new Soldiers with an invitation to become an active part of our FRG "Family." It was amazing to see this idea snowball as new spouses started to get involved very quickly simply because they had been welcomed and made to feel special.

The Green Plate was also delivered to wounded warriors recovering at Walter Reed Medical Center in the fall of 2009 as friends and family donated books and spouse groups baked to fill plates with cookies. This simple reminder that we "do remember" brought many smiles and some tears to eyes of Soldiers who were visited by strangers so they would know that they are appreciated and not forgotten.

Individuals continue to request books and plates (green plastic plates offered with the book, which read "It is more blessed to give than receive...Pass it on.") They give them to new spouses in the neighborhood or to anyone who needs encouragement to get out and make the most of people, places, and life.

The Green Plate is an encouragement and a reminder that you should cherish the time you are given and encourage others to do the same. Pass it on.

–JILL CONNETT, military spouse,
 author of *The Green Plate* and *Camouflage Prayers*

417. Family pictures, especially those that include uniforms, dog tags, and American flags

Photo by Marianne Marshall Photography

418. Absence makes the heart grow fonder

*My mother-in-law, Naomi Hightower, always said to us,
"You two don't have time to get tired of each other—
you are always saying good-bye or saying hello."*

–KATHIE

My husband wrote me a letter before he left. He kept repeating that he wished that he could take all of my pain away …

You spend most of the deployment hoping for time to fly. When they are home, for that brief period, you pray for it to stop. The time together is never enough. It took us only days to fit back into our routine again. We had our family back together. The stress was lifted and the joy had returned. My best friend was lying next to me every night and he was there again every morning. I treasured every moment.

I am constantly amazed at how he can be here in the moment, knowing he has to leave again. Remaining aloof and detached would make his hurt so much less, but our time together would have been affected. I am so glad he chose to be here with us even though I know the joy of being completely and totally *here* means the pain of leaving will be even harder for him.

Taking him back to the airport and coming home alone was excruciating. I wish that he could take my pain away and that I could take his pain away, too. I do, but I don't. I don't because on my way home, through the horrible feeling in my gut, the tears that wouldn't stop, the sleep I couldn't find, and the ache in my heart I realized that pain was the feeling of being in love, the pain of being alive—the feeling of an emotion some don't ever experience. I love him. He loves me. Totally and completely. I don't want the pain, but I'll take it if it means I get to live a life full of that kind of love.

–TARA

419. Resilience training or deployment prep

Positive psychology tools to aid Service members and families in their ability to grow and thrive in the face of challenges and to bounce back from the impact of deployments

★ ★

Child-Care Assistance

420. Child Development Centers

421. SitterCity.com/DoD

422. Family in-home child-care centers, evaluated for you

423. List of installation-certified babysitters (and free training to certify them)

424. Free child care for many volunteer positions

425. Free respite care for families caring for an exceptional family member through the Exceptional Family Member Program (EFMP)

★ ★

426. Youth service centers and programs

427. Teen centers

428. Assistance programs at the DoD and Service levels
- **Military One Source** www.militaryonesource.com
- **Air Force Combat Support & Community Service** www.usafservices.com
- **Army OneSource** www.myarmyonesource.com
- **Army Reserve Family Programs** www.arfp.org
- **National Guard Bureau Joint Services Support** www.jointservicessupport.org
- **Coast Guard Work-Life Programs** www.uscg.mil/worklife
- **Marine Corps Community Services** www.usmc-mccs.org
- **Navy Fleet and Family Support Program** www.nffsp.org

429. Military Family Research Institute

430. Pride gear like camouflaged handbags for spouses or "I'm a Navy Dad" and other similar sweatshirts for parents

431. The deep joy when you are able to be a part of extended-family holiday gatherings—a joy that much sweeter because the opportunity is so rare

432. Health care and dental coverage
    It requires paperwork but it's available and low cost

433. Soaking up the local customs
    How many people can say they've been to the Rattlesnake Rodeo in Alabama, the Daffodil Festival in Washington, the Seafood Festival in Georgia, and/or the Garlic Fest in California?

434. The wonderful opportunities to have your child attend a DoD school or international school while living overseas

435. Watching your child graduate from high school in a castle in Germany or in ancient ruins in Turkey

436. Having your kids understand the responsibilities of citizenship in this country

437. The fun of hanging Christmas tree ornaments with memories of each place you have lived

"That sunflower one is from our time at Fort Leavenworth, Kansas; the raindrop is from Joint Base Lewis-McChord, Washington; the nutcracker is of course from Germany." And who else would have a miniature Marine or Soldier complete with rucksack, rifle, and dog tag on their tree?

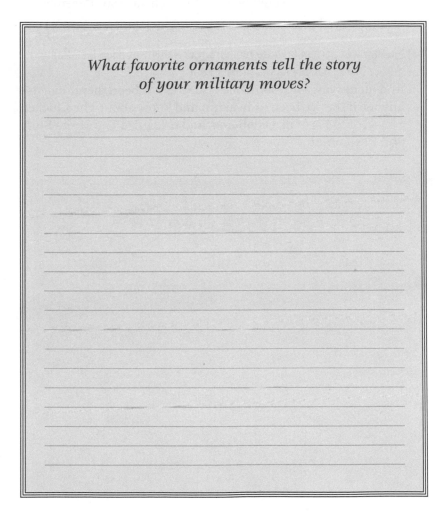

What favorite ornaments tell the story of your military moves?

438. Military kids, no matter the Service, embracing the positive parts of change—what an incredible life lesson to learn so young!

439. New holiday traditions you adopt as your own family traditions because of experiences in different parts of the world
    * The practice of Advent calendars
    * Hiding the pickle in the Christmas tree
    * Coal or candy in your shoes on St. Nicholas Day, December 6
    * Black-eyed peas and grits for good luck on New Year's Day

440. Finding that perfect favorite restaurant or activity at each installation—burger joints, holiday lights, breweries
    And identifying with someone else who has been there. Just ask anyone if they've been to Iwakuni and know about The Chicken Shack, or to Fort Sill, Oklahoma, and recognize The Meers Store and Restaurant.

What favorites do you have?

441. **Taking advantage of each Service branch and installation's local recreation areas**

★ A wonderfully outfitted "double-wide" vacation home on Whidbey Island, Washington

★ Enjoying a big family reunion renting two houses right on the beach at Air Force Bellows Beach in Hawaii, with the convenience and affordability of groceries and other supplies from the Marine Corps base at Kaneohe Bay just twenty minutes away

★ A warm Thanksgiving gathering of family renting campsites on the beach in San Diego through Camp Pendleton in California

★ Staying in an oceanfront cottage at Oak Grove Park Beach on Pensacola's Naval Air Station, Florida

★ Snuggling up in a cozy log cabin on American Lake at Joint Base Lewis-McChord, Washington

442. **Movie theaters on military installations**

443. **Overseas assignments—not just Germany or Japan, but Greece, The Bahamas, or Spain**

444. **The joy found in throwing together a last-minute Halloween or school play costume from odds and ends of old uniform pieces**

445. **"Military 101" programs to help military spouses learn the ropes**
   • Air Force Heart Link
   • Army Family Team Building
   • Navy COMPASS Program
   • Marine Corps L.I.N.K.S.—Lifestyle, Insights, Networking, Knowledge, and Skills

446. **Watching the "paper chain" of deployment days getting shorter**

447. **Eating Thanksgiving dinner "with the troops" in a Mess Hall/Dining Facility—all those men and women in dress uniforms**

448. School Liaison Officers (SLOs)

449. Drinking exotic coffee and tea
Enjoy a formal and fascinating tea ceremony in Japan, grab a can (yes, a can) of hot coffee from a vending machine in a Japanese railroad station, or have some Kaffee und Kuchen with friends and family in Germany.

450. Military recreation centers
Affordable joint service hotels/resorts managed by the U.S. military to provide vacation opportunities to all Service members and their families

★ Staying at the beautiful Hale Koa, a first class hotel right in the middle of Hawaii's Waikiki beach, an amazing seventy-two acres of tropical oasis, for military only

★ Skiing in Garmisch, Germany, and enjoying your stay at the Edelweiss Lodge and Resort

★ Staying at Shades of Green while exploring Disney World

★ Enjoying the sunrise at Cape Henry Inn and Beach Club on the Chesapeake Bay in Virginia

★ A vacation at MC Memorial Club and Hotel in San Francisco, California

★ Staying at the New Sanno Hotel located in downtown Tokyo, Japan

★ The experience of Dragon Hill Lodge in Seoul, South Korea

> *It is a tremendous blessing to experience the warmth, hospitality, and generosity of the Korean people.*
> *Plus, it is a marvel to experience hopping on the subway in the very modern and densely populated city of Seoul, and hopping off an hour later to hike stupendous mountains in the middle of the outlying countryside.*
>
> –CATHY STERLING

What were your favorite military family vacation experiences?

451. Privatized housing on military installations
Providing improved military housing in a timelier manner and with more services than the military could provide. Those of us who've lived in many of the older, and in some cases truly substandard, military housing know what a difference this has made in many areas.

To find out more about privatized housing and the Military Housing Privatization Initiative (MHPI), visit www.acq.osd.mil/housing/mhpi.htm.

452. Armed Forces Vacation Club (AFVC) at www.afvclub.com
A "space available" program that offers all active and retired members of the Armed Forces and DoD-affiliated personnel the opportunity to enjoy vacations at more than 3,500 resorts, apartments, condominiums, and homes in more than eighty countries at an incredible value. Although accommodations are mostly at time-share resorts, you are not required to attend a time-share presentation nor are there any membership fee requirements in order to take advantage of these incredible deals.

453. Basic Allowance for Housing (BAH)—tax free

454. Support and awareness "runs" or 5Ks/10Ks

455. A "military rate" or "government rate" at many hotels

456. Welcome-home ceremonies
The men and women of the ship standing tall in their sharp dress uniforms scanning the faces on the pier. The Soldiers, Airmen, or Marines, in formation, marching across the field all dressed in their battle gear, hoping to soon be released to the cheering crowd. There is nothing that can describe the sense of pride and the quantity of tears when taking part in the reunion of a unit returning from deployment.

457. The "Christmas-like" joy of opening boxes you've had in storage and discovering your treasures all over again

458. Flying Space A—the thrill of the unexpected!

When you have the leave/liberty time (or are retired), pack your bags, collect your IDs/passports, head to the Air Mobility Command (AMC) terminal closest to you, and just get on the next plane with space available—who knows where your next vacation adventure will be? Wherever they fly to, that's where you will go. There are forty-two AMC passenger terminals throughout the world: United States, Northwest Pacific, Southwest Pacific, Indian Ocean, Europe, and North Africa. Why not?

Check out Air Mobility Command at www.amc.af.mil/amctravel/index.asp for all Space-A information and a terminal nearest you.

> Kathie and I often talk about the group of women we met when we did a workshop at Travis AFB, California. Their spouses were all retired military. They told us that often on a Friday evening they would all show up at the AMC terminal with a small bag packed. Three couples who've been longtime friends. If they could all get out on a flight, they'd hop on, no matter where it was going. If they couldn't, they'd go out to dinner together and then try another day. What fun. Made us think we should retire right near an AMC terminal.
>
> –HOLLY

459. The last night before deployment

Your heart aches, but so much joy can be found in loving someone so much that you'll miss them so fiercely.

460. Military guest lodging or temporary housing

Low-cost accommodations in virtually any major metropolitan area. *Military Travel Guide* U.S.A., published by Military Living, lists phone numbers and websites for temporary lodging facilities in the United States.

Fort Knox by Paul Jon

461. Reinventing the holidays by crafting unique family holiday memories necessitated by military life

From a "flat" spouse at the Thanksgiving table to your spouse joining the celebration via Skype. Or maybe it'll be Christmas in June because you're celebrating before or after deployment.

> Our son Darren painted a self-portrait in one of his college art classes. When he was deployed, we used his self-portrait in all our family photos. We even propped it up at the Christmas dinner table. We took photos of him with us and sent them to him, just to let him know we thought of him at that time when families are normally together. Crazy? Maybe, but it worked for us during the separation.
>
> –ROZ RILEY, Army brat, Army veteran, Army wife, Army mom

462. Outdoor recreation rentals

★ Renting ocean kayaks from Joint Base Pearl Harbor-Hickam and kayaking off Hickam Beach in Hawaii

★ Renting fishing gear in Washington state courtesy of Joint Base Lewis-McChord

★ Camping in an RV and hiking on Mount Scott through Fort Sill, Oklahoma

463. Inexpensive Servicemembers' Group Life Insurance (SGLI)

464. Running into someone you knew at another assignment and rekindling the relationship

465. The instant connection you feel with other military families

466. The anticipation of arriving at a new place
"Wonder who my new best friend will be here; wonder what the new house will be like; wonder what new adventures we'll have here."

467. Welcome-home convoys
There is nothing like the experience of those military buses all convoying together as the flag-waving crowd ushers the Service members home.

468. Commissary baggers—who work for tips only

469. The fun and adventure of family road trips
You move cross-country from one assignment to another, stopping at every historic site, eating junk food you normally do not allow. (What would a road trip be without CornNuts and strawberry licorice Twizzlers and stops at Dairy Queen for a chocolate-dipped ice cream cone?)

470. Affordable travel, tickets, and trip planning assistance
From MWR; Information, Ticketing, and Registration (ITR) office; Information, Tickets, and Travel (ITT) office; or Carlson Wagonlit Travel

★ The experience of European bus trips

★ An incredible four-day hut-to-hut hike in Austria viewing vistas in the mountains that are accessible only by foot or mountain bike

★ Exploring and enjoying fresh air on Volksmarches through the forests of Bavaria (not to mention those fun medals)

★ Affordable and accessible trips to Thailand, China, and Hong Kong from South Korea

Photo by Petty Officer 2nd Class Michael Lantron

Children sitting in a scale model of USS *Russell* to welcome the ship at Naval Station Pearl Harbor

471. Making "Welcome Home" banners

472. Family Services
- **Family Advocacy Program**
- **Exceptional Family Member Program**
- **Financial Readiness Program**—Free classes and one-on-one help for managing your money; classes in investing, getting rid of debt, budgeting, saving, and retirement planning
- **Life skills**—Education in parenting, stress management, and other issues
- **Relocation assistance**—To help families move and adapt to a new location

473. The fun of driving around a new installation in the housing area, reading the name signs to see if there is anyone you already know

474. Commissary privileges—the savings, especially on meats and basics
Civilians call them grocery stores. We call ours Commissaries.

THE COMMISSARY
It's not just the name that's different!

★

- You can't shop at a Commissary without an ID card. You can use your Service ID card to shop at any other Service commissary.

- Commissaries are nonprofit organizations. By law, Commissaries are required to sell goods at prices that are set at a level to recover the cost of goods, with no profit built into these prices.

- The Defense Commissary Agency (DeCA) proudly boasts a 30 percent annual savings over your typical local grocery store bill. And you can save more using coupons.

- There is a required, Congress-mandated surcharge (currently 5%) to pay for Commissary construction, equipment, and continually improved facilities. The amount of surcharge applied to a Commissary sale transaction is shown as "SCG" on your sales receipt. The surcharge is applied to the total value of your order *before* coupon values are deducted.

- Like traditional grocery or "big box" stores, Commissaries accept most types of coupons in accordance with the terms and conditions stated on a coupon to make items even more affordable.

Note: Commissaries located in overseas areas accept coupons up to six months after the expiration date stated on a coupon. Commissaries also accept Internet or home-printed coupons provided they meet certain criteria. Even better, each commissary hosts a "coupon board" or stand when you enter the building, where they offer coupons that you can use immediately.

- Commissaries frequently hold events where you can purchase goods at an even greater discount. In May and October of each year, DeCA runs a truckload or case lot sale—at all Commissaries.

- DeCA is so committed to its members' satisfaction that they'll take special orders. Contact a member of management to request a certain item (by UPC code) to be carried. If you are not sure of the UPC code, bring the empty box with you. They can tell you instantly if the item is on the authorized list. The Commissary ... It's Worth the Trip!

475. Trick-or-treating in the stairwells in Europe
So many doors in a short time without having to go outside

476. Education centers

477. Junior Reserve Officer Training Corps (JROTC)
Teaching patriotism, leadership, and responsibility to teens

> I've visited JROTC programs all over the country, from robust public schools in economically strong towns to programs in Watts, California, and New Orleans with metal detectors at every door and police on staff patrolling the school halls. I've visited schools in places like Guam, Tinian, and American Samoa. In all of the programs, I observed students stepping into positions of responsibility and leadership, demonstrating their skills with pride. In some of those schools, the JROTC program was the first time these young men and women had been taught the concept of respect, not only for others, but for themselves. In some of those schools, JROTC was the only light at the end of the tunnel.
>
> –GREG HIGHTOWER, retired U.S. Army Lieutenant Colonel

478. The sense of freedom and fun of living without your things for a time
Once the packers have packed and hauled everything away to move to your next duty station

479. Sharing our holiday traditions with friends from other countries
Such as making them a traditional Thanksgiving meal (the only "truly American" meal)

480. Hearing from a friend on Facebook about their life "back home"
It makes you realize the enormous amount of experience you have gained from being part of the military and "leaving home"

481. Phrases with which we are all very familiar
Next, please!

Now serving C325 at window number two.

ID, please.

Sponsor's last four?

482. Fourth of July picnics on the installation

Lying on blankets under the stars with a real cannon being shot off as part of the "1812 Overture"

483. Learning how to better handle a move

Figuring out new systems of what works—like walking behind movers and marking details on each box or videotaping your goods before packing them ... then feeling that sense of pride in knowing what to do. (Even if it only comes after about ten moves!)

484. Inviting a foreign military student to a Christmas tree decorating party

It opens up interesting discussions of beliefs and customs around the world

485. Homecoming—especially the Kodak moments

The first embrace, all the new babies meeting their daddies, and proud and relieved parents

Photo by Petty Officer 3rd Class Brian Goodwin

486. Reading your new installation's newspaper
To learn what's different at this location and the thrill of discovering what your newest home has to offer
- What is the Exchange like?
- Does this Commissary have more to offer than the last?
- What classes are available at the fitness center?
- What outdoor recreation programs are unique to this area that you've never experienced before?

487. Block parties/summer BBQ

488. The Exchange
Price match policy, Military Star Card, tax-free shopping, and free shipping via the website

489. Incredible medical centers and cutting-edge research
- National Naval Medical Center—Bethesda, Maryland
- Brooke Army Medical Center—San Antonio, Texas
- Landstuhl Regional Medical Center—Germany
- Tripler Army Medical Center—Honolulu, Hawaii
- Madigan Army Medical Center—Tacoma, Washington
- Walter Reed Medical Center—Washington, D.C., transitioning to DeWitt Army Community Hospital at Fort Belvoir, Virginia, in 2011

490. "Quarters Sweet Quarters"

491. Joint Family Support Assistance Program (JFSAP)
Provides outreach and assistance to military families who are geographically isolated from installation resources
See www.militaryhomefront.dod.mil/sp/jfsap.

492. Lending closets

493. Military-speak or lingo
Immediately understanding terms that civilians don't know

494. Shopping in foreign exchanges on multinational bases

495. Getting to know your own country as some never will

★ Scenic ocean views from Tyndall Air Force Base, Florida, to the Presidio of Monterey, California: Paradise by the Sea

★ Living at the foot of Pike's Peak, "America's Mountain," whether you're at Fort Carson, the Air Force Academy, or Peterson Air Force Base, Colorado

★ Niagara Falls, New York—an Air Reserve Station and a natural wonder

★ Stepping out into the crisp cold air of an early morning at Fort Irwin, California, to be greeted by the immensity of the sky out in that desert location—and blown away by the stars at night with so few lights to compete

★ Saving lives just a stone's throw from the San Antonio, Texas, River Walk. Remember the Alamo!

★ The shock of being issued a snow blower when stationed and living in post housing at Fort Drum, New York

★ Living in Alaska and watching mama and baby moose in the backyard, bear in the front, bald eagles in the skies, rafts of otters, two-hundred-plus-pound halibut, and other wildlife in the waters

★ Being a part of an outrigger forty-mile relay race in Hawaii

★ The magic of a parade at Joint Base Lewis-McChord, Washington, with Mount Rainier at the end of the parade field in all its glory—and the shock when you first step out one morning and find that Mount Rainier has "simply disappeared" even though it doesn't look overcast

496. Having Commissary access to a great selection of German, Korean, Japanese, and other foods that you developed a taste for overseas
Some in small rural communities where you wouldn't otherwise be able to find such ethnic/specialty foods

497. Hobby shop—arts and crafts

You Know You Are a Service Member When ...

You watch the world news or the travel channel and often find yourself saying, "I was deployed there" or "I was stationed there."

498. Getting to know the world as some never will

★ Enjoying a French canal barge trip, a short drive from assignments in Germany, made affordable by driving the barge yourself and cooking meals from local market purchases

★ Climbing the hundreds of steps to the top of a ziggurat in the southern Iraqi city of Ur, which is believed to be Abraham's birthplace and holy land

★ Attending a midnight Mass at Christmas in one of the great cathedrals of Europe

★ Going to Lourdes, France, on a military-chaplain-run trip

★ Running a marathon on the Great Wall of China, a convenient trip from Okinawa

499. Laughing and sharing humor as a way to cope with this life, by comics who have lived this life

• **Mollie Gross,** former U.S. Marine Corps spouse, comedian

• **Juan Canopii,** former U.S. Airman, actor and comedian

• **Trevor Romain,** former U.S. Army paratrooper, comedian

• **Jan Donahue,** U.S. Army spouse and mother, comedian

500. Historical (and sometimes rather hysterical) housing

501. Listening to helpful talk radio shows by military families
- *Army Wife Talk Radio* www.armywifenetwork.com
- *Christian Military Wife Radio* www.christianmilitarywives.com
- *Navy Wife Radio* www.mymilitarylife.com/radio

"After spending two sea tours and a shore tour on the waterfront, we PCS'd to the middle of the country in 2007," says Wendy Poling, Navy spouse and founder of Navy Wife Radio. "For the first time I felt isolated and thought, 'There has to be a way to connect with other military spouses who feel the same way,' so I created a military blog. Back then the military spouse online community was very small. The Navy Wife Radio show grew out of that need to connect us all in an even closer way. My goal is to motivate and encourage military spouses to do what they love and follow their dreams."

Navy Wife Radio, originally a podcast of SubmarineWife.com, was started later in 2007. The show has grown from its infancy of twenty-five listeners to thousands and found its home at MyMilitaryLife.com, which concentrates on joint-service content.

"Since our show is a podcast, our listeners include spouses from all around the world including Japan, Germany, and Hawaii. I recently traveled to Hawaii and what an amazing treat it was to actually meet listeners in person!" Wendy said.

Wendy has been joined by cohost Marla Barlow, also a military spouse, and a team of spouses who help produce the show and write the blog.

Wendy credits the team's efforts for the popularity of the show and success of the website.

Want to tune in? Search *Navy Wife Radio* or *Military Life Radio* on iTunes to subscribe to the podcast. You can also listen by visiting their website at www.mymilitarylife.com/radio or live at www.blogtalkradio.com/navywiferadio most Tuesdays at 9 p.m. EST.

502. The appreciation of a holiday or anniversary that is celebrated together

503. The excitement you feel when someone you're talking to says he or she has been to the same post or base you have

504. Unit-level and intramural sports programs

505. Celebrating traditional festivals with our host nations

506. A wait in the emergency room shorter than six hours

507. No good-byes—just "see you later"—it's a small military

When I was in my forties, a guy about my age walked up to me while I was standing in line at the Heidelberg, Germany, mail room. He said, "Hey, I know you. We must have been stationed together." This not being an uncommon experience, we immediately began exchanging assignments and deployments we'd had over the years. Quickly we discovered that neither of us had ever been stationed or deployed to the same place at the same time. Finally, while talking about our lives overall, we realized where we knew each other from. Thirty years ago we were on the same Little League baseball team when we were eleven years old and our dads were stationed in Tachikawa, Japan. Now that is a small world!

–GREG HIGHTOWER

★ ★

Creative Ways to Cope and Stay Connected During Separation

508. CamoSock at www.camosock.com

CamoSock is a creation of Terk Designs LLC. The military Christmas stocking was designed to become a true keepsake for the Soldier, Marine, Sailor, Airman, or Coast Guardsman who receives one. They are made of fabric identical to the corresponding uniform, with colored piping. Use them as holiday gifts themselves, or add some goodies to make them the perfect HGDS: Holiday Gift Delivery System. Displaying the stocking will become a wonderful addition to any family's Christmas holiday traditions.

509. Troops-in-Touch at www.createmygift.com/troops-in-touch

This not-for-profit project gives children the ability to make art-based activities their own, offering them engaging ways to express their feelings and emotions.

510. Hug A Hero/Daddy Dolls at www.operationhugahero.com or www.daddydolls.com

Tricia Dyal cofounded Daddy Dolls Inc., also known as Hug A Hero, with Nikki Darnell in 2005. The wife of an active-duty Marine and mother to two precious daughters, Dyal saw the need to provide extra comfort for her children while their father was deployed overseas. Daddy Dolls are a head-to-toe photo of your Service member dyed onto a soft, huggable, washable, microfiber fabric that can be personalized with your child's name. The dolls are offered in small, large, and "BIG Daddy" sizes.

511. Flat Stanley at www.flatstanley.com

Jeff Brown wrote the book *Flat Stanley* in 1964, the first in a series about a totally flat boy. When Stanley gets flattened by the

Photo by Kaawaloa Kekauoha Taylor

Army Capt. Michael W. Taylor with "Flat Mika" (after his son) in Camp Spann, Afghanistan

Photo by Kyla Sikorski

"Daddy dolls" of Army Capt. Tim Sikorski at home with his daughter Luella while he was deployed to Iraq

Photo by Paula Schapp

Army Sgt. 1st Class Josh Schapp at home in "flat daddy" form while he served in Afghanistan

fall of a large bulletin board, he starts new adventures, like sliding under doors. He discovers he can now visit friends by being mailed to them in an envelope.

In 1995, Dale Hubert created The Flat Stanley project, inviting teachers and students to take part. The concept is to create a flat visitor that can travel in an envelope. The receiver then takes the flat visitor and travels with it, taking pictures and writing about their adventures. For military families, this can be a great way to stay connected—send a flat child on an adventure with his or her parent overseas, or take pictures and write about a flat parent's participation in events back home.

512. Flat Daddy at www.flatdaddies.com

These life-size printed posters of parents who are actively serving overseas in the military are printed on a rollable, adhesive-backed material and are delivered unmounted. The Flat Daddy program is made possible by SFC Graphics in Toledo, Ohio. But the flat daddy had military spouse beginnings.

The book *I'm Already Home … Again* by Elaine Dumler captures a story of Cindy and her nineteen-month-old daughter Sarah. Sarah's dad deployed and Cindy took a picture of him in his uniform to a local print shop and asked for it to be enlarged to life size. She mounted it on foam board. Flat Daddy then traveled to graduations, weddings, and other celebrations. He appeared in many photos and they sent copies to Sarah's dad overseas so he could see the places he had been. Flat Daddy can be "made into" many others: Flat Hubby, Flat Wifey, Flat Mommy, Flat Hottie, Flat Honey, Flat Baby, Flat Pet, or Flat Brat.

> *When I got my daughter's flat daddy in the mail,*
> *I wasn't quite sure what to do with it. It took me a week*
> *to decide. It was kind of hard for her to carry it, but she*
> *wanted him to go everywhere with her. So I made it into*
> *a backpack! She loves that she can carry him anywhere*
> *and not worry about tripping or falling over. Thank you*
> *so much! She can love on him anytime she wants …*
> *This has made one little girl very happy!*
>
> –SONYA PREDMORE, Army spouse

513. Huggee Miss You Dolls through Operation Give a Hug at www.operationgiveahug.org

Huggee Miss You Dolls were created by Audrey Storch, a breast cancer survivor. While she was hospitalized, her sons would go to bed with her photo clutched in their hands, crumpling them in the night. Audrey created dolls with a plastic sleeve to slip her photo into. The idea spread, people started asking for them, and a business developed.

Army spouse Susan Agustin discovered the dolls when relatives sent one to her three-year-old daughter, Maddie, with photos of her cousins to keep in front of her.

"When my husband, Gene, deployed to Qatar, Daddy's photo replaced the cousins," says Susan. "The doll went everywhere with Maddie. In fact, Gene would call and ask, 'Where did we go and what did we do today?' "

Seeing the positive impact of the doll, Agustin created the nonprofit Operation Give a Hug in 2004 and worked on fundraising so that all military children who needed them could have dolls. Since its inception, Operation Give a Hug has given more than 315,000 dolls to children of Service members. The dolls are also being used by pediatric psychologists and school counselors to help children cope with deployment. For military families the dolls come in digital camouflage with voice recording.

514. United Through Reading at www.unitedthroughreading.org

Long-lasting memories are created by a deployed Mom or Dad reading books while being recorded. The DVD is sent to the child, who can watch it and even read along.

★ ★

What are your favorite creative ways to cope and stay connected during separation?

Photo by Dustin Senger

Army Sgt. Anthony Henderson makes a video from the USO lounge at Camp As Sayliyah, Qatar.

515. Holidays celebrated with your spouse or extended family via webcam

516. Free e-mail accounts with instant messaging (IM) and video messaging through Knowledge Online

517. Discounted veterinary services on military installations

518. Military Family Life Consultants—free counseling if you need it

519. Thrift shops

520. The comfort you feel when someone tells you they've been to the same assignment or unit you are going to. What a jump start!

> *At our AWN Spouse Field Exercise events, one of our ice breaker items is to find someone who has been to a place where you've been stationed. I love to watch the attendees' faces light up when they find a match—there is an instant bond.*
>
> –TARA

521. Family Readiness Programs and groups

Command-sponsored programs to link families with Service members' chains of command

Virtual Family Support programs are also becoming available, like the one at www.armyfrg.org.

522. Helpful publications for military families
   - *Family,* the magazine for military families
   - *Foundations,* National Guard Soldier and Family magazine
   - *Military Money* online magazine
   - *Military Spouse* magazine
   - *On Patrol,* the magazine of the USO
   - *The Patriot,* the official magazine of Fisher House Foundation

You Know You Are a Military Spouse When ...

You start reading *[Military] Times* instead of *Cosmopolitan*

523. Army Family Action Plan (AFAP) and its impact on all Services

Have you ever had one of those moments where you think, "There has to be a better way"? The Army Family Action Plan program is a great example of spouses asking for change for all of us. AFAP began because Army spouses organized in order to improve the quality of life for all Army families. Army spouse Joyce Ott convinced the Army to have the first Army Family Symposium, which continues today as AFAP.

Every year through AFAP, community members at every post get to raise top concerns, asking for what they want changed. Many of those issues are solved locally. Others are taken to the Department of Army level. In fact, since the program started in 1983, no fewer than 95 changes have been made to legislation, 137 revisions made to policy and regulations, and 153 programs or services improved. You may recognize some of these improvements as the Thrift Savings Plan (TSP), SGLI increasing from $50,000 to $400,000, BAH increasing by 11 percent as part of a COLA package, and FSA increasing from $75 to $100 per month.

> **DID YOU KNOW?**
>
> The Army may be the only Service branch to have such a program, but 52 percent of AFAP issues benefit all of the Department of Defense, not just the Army. Things have changed for the better for all of us—because someone suggested a better way!

524. Operation: Military Kids at www.operationmilitarykids.org

Connects military children and youth with local resources to give them a sense of community support and to enhance their well-being

525. APO, FPO, and SPO mail—big savings when living or mailing overseas

Also I love the great mail order companies that ship to APOs ... they make life in [South] Korea a bit easier!

–DONNA WINZENRIED, Army wife, Army mom, and advocate for military families

526. Free tax preparation

527. Getting letters from Santa c/o Elmendorf Air Force Base, Alaska

528. Military children's books

Books to help both kids and parents identify with other "military brats" who are both encountering similar challenges and reaping the benefits of a military life

- *A Heart Apart,* a customizable book by Melissa Seligman and Christina Piper
- *I'm a Hero Too* by Jenny Sokol
- *Military Kids Speak* by Julie Rahm
- *Sammy's Soldier* by Sarah White
- *Uncle Sam's Kids* by Angela Sportelli-Rehak
- *We Serve Too! and We Serve Too! 2* by Kathleen Edick and Paula Johnson

I owe everything to my military upbringing. It made me the man and the athlete I am today.

–SHAQUILLE O'NEAL

What are your favorite military children's books?

529. Military Youth on the Move at www.defenselink.mil/mtom
Designed to help youth with relocations

> I have lived at Plattsburgh AFB, New York; Fairchild AFB, Washington; Pease AFB, New Hampshire; Portales, New Mexico; New Richmond, Wisconsin; and Eau Claire, Wisconsin; and I currently live in Minneapolis, where I attend the University of Minnesota. Throughout my travels I have attended two elementary schools, one middle school, one junior high, two high schools, and three universities, despite the fact that I am only a sophomore.
>
> I feel sorry for the civilian kids I went to high school with. They all want to settle down in the same area that they grew up in. That's definitely not for me. I've tasted the world, and I want to gobble it up. There are so many places that I want to go and see before I leave this world. There just isn't enough time.
>
> Life would be boring otherwise.
>
> –JENNIFER SIERACKI, on Militarybratlife.com

530. Hooah 4 Health at www.hooah4health.com
An Army health promotion and wellness website targeted for the Reserve components, covering health in the body, mind, spirit, and environment

531. Military Child Education Coalition at www.militarychild.org
A group focused on ensuring quality education opportunities for all military children affected by mobility, family separation, and transition

532. Lines
Laugh if you will, but nobody can form a line and wait like the military

533. Receiving your household goods

534. Freedom walks

535. The "fun" of taking your German driving test
Often needing to take it more than once to pass, but giggling like a little kid at the Autobahn signs, especially "Gute Fahrt!"

536. Marriage-enrichment retreats
- **Air Force Marriage Care weekends, post-deployment**
- **Army chaplain-led Strong Bonds program**
- **AUSA Family Programs and Stronger Families' "Oxygen for Your Relationship" seminars**
- **Navy, Marine, and Coast Guard marriage enrichment retreats through CREDO**

I wasn't sure what I expected when I walked through the doors of the hotel and into the Strong Bonds retreat weekend. Part of me believed it stood little chance to make a great impact in our marriage. We are fairly decent when it comes to communication. We have been through the challenge of deployment/redeployment three times. We are in counseling.

We "check in" with each other in terms of goals, dreams, and languages of love. We focus on each other ... What could a piece of paper, a PowerPoint, or even two days revolving around trust really do for us that three deployments hadn't done? ...

As I sat at the table the first night, taking in the couples around me, I began to realize I wasn't alone. As we sat in small groups, eating the first meal of many, the lady across from me texted, her lips pursed out and her body language solid. Her husband had his arm around her, but her stance was stiff, her eyes rolled. I felt that familiar stare, that all-too-tense state of "don't come too close. The remnants of a deployment are dripping off me."

To my right, I saw other couples. Timid in gesture. Looking around to see what others were doing ... I wanted to know their stories. Know what they had been through. Know why they had come to a marriage retreat.

And that is when it hit me: I was seeking out all these answers, silently questioning these couples, because I needed something. But I still wasn't sure what it was.

That first night, we went to bed still questioning. "What do you think?" I asked him.

"I'm not sure yet. I really like the idea of having a weekend focused on just us. I like that the kids have great child care. We'll see."

... The next morning, as we sat, again, across from strangers and vaguely familiar faces, I saw it again: the nervousness. Those "what's next?" questions of all of us. But there was something new there. Something electric.

As we walked through the issues, talking about trust, marriage, communication vs. deployments, people spoke out. Ideas began to flow … And as each person spoke, heads nodded. Others leaned in for a loving whisper. A shared moment of understanding.

And just like that, people began to open their posture. Uncrossing their arms. Opening fingers to accept the wayward searching hands of their partners. You could feel love pulsing in that conference room …

As we broke into groups, women and men, and discussed trust, roles, and sex, I saw more women sneaking looks across the room, meeting the eyes of their husbands. Lingering there. Their lips turning slightly into an impish grin and knowing flirtation. A "come hither" spark sent across the room.

That was when it hit me: what I needed.

We are inundated daily with stories of failing marriages. Divorce. Abuse. Shots fired in anger. My heart sinks every time the media moves toward the story of woe. The painful burr. The horrific fear of what "could" happen. But rarely do we see running stories and headlines of another story. The one that is rarely told. And the one I obviously had been hoping to hear:

"Military couples seeking ways to fight for their marriage. Pushing against the statistics and past the desire to just give up."

I needed to see that fight … the one that said, "I'm worn out. Busted. Broken. And I feel like I can't take another step. But I still deeply love you. And I won't quit."

I needed to feel that electricity of the fight. The we-aren't-perfect-but-we-are-perfectly-trying fight … I needed to be immersed in it. Needed to know I wasn't alone. And that many, many other couples are searching for a way through.

It could have ended for me with the awkward beginning silences. The unwillingness to talk about all our issues. Instead, for me, it began there.

Once again, I sat in awe as I watched military couples lead. Through speaking. Through honesty. And through true unity. The seed of "togetherness." The feeling that no matter how much mud we wade through, no matter how much sometimes I just want to walk out the door, there is another person who understands. Hears me. And fights for her marriage right beside me.

–MELISSA SELIGMAN, Army wife, author of *The Day after He Left for Iraq*, cofounder of HerWarHerVoice.com

537. U.S. Army Soldier Show and Air Force Tops in Blue

538. Military bumper stickers

    Half my heart is in … Iraq, Afghanistan, the Military

    You Are Not Forgotten … POW-MIA

    Official Military Ribbons and Seals

    My other car is a … Humvee, tank, submarine, jet

    All Gave Some. Some Gave All.

    Proud Parent of a(n) … Airman, Soldier, Coastie, Sailor, or Marine

    I may look harmless, but I raised a U.S. Marine

What's on the back of your
car, truck, van, or SUV?

Photo by Jhomil Bansil

Santa visits Peterson AFB for his NORAD mission brief in preparation for Christmas Eve.

539. Tracking Santa on Christmas Eve with NORAD at www.noradsanta.org

The NORAD Tracks Santa program began in 1955 after a phone call to the Continental Air Defense Command Operations Center in Colorado Springs, Colorado. The call was from a local youngster who dialed a misprinted telephone number in a local newspaper advertisement. The commander on duty who answered the phone that night gave the youngster the information requested—the whereabouts of Santa. This began the tradition of tracking Santa, a tradition that was carried on by NORAD when it was formed in 1958. The NORAD Tracks Santa program has grown immensely since first presented on the Internet in 1998. The website receives millions of unique visitors from hundreds of countries and territories around the world. In addition, a live Operations Center is occupied for twenty-five hours with more than twelve hundred volunteers each year who receive hundreds of thousands of phone calls and e-mails from families around the world. Even First Lady Michelle Obama volunteered her time on December 24, 2010.

See more at www.norad.mil.

You Know You Are a Military Spouse When ...
You plan a special day because of the
prospects of a "case lot sale"

540. Case lot sales
Each year in May and September, the Defense Commissary
Agency holds a worldwide case lot sale event, offering customers
bulk quantities, at increased savings, of their favorite products,
such as canned goods, beverages, cleaning or laundry products,
and, in some cases, fresh chicken, pork, beef, and produce. The
sales occur at stores on military installations around the world
throughout September.

To find out when your store is hosting a sale, check out
Commissaries.com or ask at your local Commissary.

541. Term of endearment—"military brats"
And backronyms: "Born, Raised and Transferred" or "Brave,
Resilient, Adaptable, and Trustworthy"

542. Furniture pieces that have seen duty in just about every type of room
From living room to dining room to bedroom, based on avail-
able space

**543. Ending up at the same place many years later and the fun of discovering
what's new and what hasn't changed at all**

544. Free SAT or ACT preparatory programs for military families
Subsidized through donations from organizations like Victory
Sports Group (professional football players)

545. Traveling overseas and experiencing all of the different cuisines
Nothing like German Käsespätzle, Japanese mochi, Korean
Be Bim Bop, or Belgian moules frites!

546. Driving the German Autobahn

547. Military specialty license plates
Like those that recognize Veterans, National Guard and Reserve members, former POWs, Purple Heart recipients, and Pearl Harbor survivors

548. Free relocation services

549. Installation libraries

550. MilitaryByOwner.com, a company that provides advertising support to military families trying to sell or rent their homes

551. Sharing memories of bases/posts that have since closed down

552. Watching the Super Bowl, World Series, or the Oscars in the middle of the night because of the time difference in Europe, the Pacific, or Iraq and Afghanistan

553. Free workshops/programs that would cost you a lot in the nonmilitary world

For example: John Gottman–based and Love Languages–based relationship workshops through Chaplain or Family Service Centers, how-to classes at the auto shops, ScreamFree Parenting workshops, Seven Habits of Highly Effective Military Families workshops, or Dave Ramsey's Financial Peace University

554. Self-Help Issue Points, where you can borrow the tools you need for free

555. Special military brat memories, such as ice skating at Rhein-Main Air Base, Germany

> *Where cute Airmen handed out rental skates*
> *—a big deal for an eleven-year-old girl!*

–KATHIE

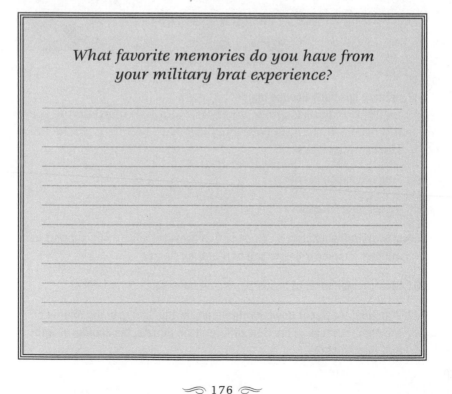

What favorite memories do you have from your military brat experience?

>>> **DID YOU KNOW?**

> According to one study of military brats by sociologist Morten Ender, more than 80 percent of brats now speak at least one language other than English and 14 percent speak three or more. His study revealed that 97 percent had lived in at least one foreign country, 63 percent in two, and 31 percent in three.

556. Foreign language classes and learning by immersion

557. Volunteers

> *When I married my high school sweetheart almost twenty years ago and he began his career in the military, I couldn't imagine the framework of my life outside our small town and family. Looking back over those years, however, I've found that my greatest achievements have been solidly rooted in my love for my family and my support for my husband's service to our nation ... Our way of life, our premise, is to serve from the inside out.*

> −DR. VIVIAN CARRASCO, National Military Family Association volunteer, military spouse, and mother of a soldier

558. Installation volunteer coordinators

> *No matter how big and powerful government gets, and the many services it provides, it can never take the place of volunteers.*

> −RONALD REAGAN

559. Yellow Ribbon rooms
Providing free Internet, webcam, and video teleconferences for military families and their deployed Service members and others separated geographically

560. Cost of childbirth is free when delivering in a military hospital— just pay for the cost of the mama's food

561. The joy of receiving Christmas letters from those you've served alongside
Even though they're now stationed all over the world, you've watched their families grow up and you feel a sense of connectedness when reading their letters of adventures only a military family would understand.

Photo by Stephanie Himel-Nelson

562. Military parents

I see the military more as a benefit to my children than a disservice. I mean, what kids do you know who don't know black from white and all play as one big family, have such pride in community, and get to relocate all over the world? Sure, I worry about deployment and separation, but kids are resilient and they learn how families and friends can stay connected and love each other despite their locations. Just like that dandelion, military children really do live the motto "bloom where you're planted."

−TARA

As parents we are experiencing the third deployment of our son, Darren. My husband and I have experienced very different feelings each time Darren has deployed. As a soldier himself, my husband was confident in the Army and Darren's unit leaders and, although concerned, felt great pride in knowing his son was going to fight for his country.

I, as his mother, was watching my child go off into hostile territory. Who would protect him? I had nurtured and protected this child, hugged him when sad, encouraged him to discover new activities and interests, and watched with amazement as he enjoyed exploring new things. A different emotion swells and dwells in a mother's heart when it is her son who marches off to battle than if it were her husband.

My husband and I did the only thing we could do—trust wholly in God. We daily claimed the promises of Psalm 91, parts of which we have posted in two locations in our home. We drew comfort from the words of David.

Darren's homecoming was filled with joy beyond description, a peace that passes understanding, and the pride that only a parent can feel. We were excited to see him, hug him, and hear of his experience—and how he, too, had placed his faith in God. And it was only with a small twinge of disappointment, but also enormous satisfaction in the way we raised him, to hear him say he "wouldn't mind going back again." He did not feel himself a hero, but humbly took satisfaction in doing his duty and helping the people, whom he came to love.

−ROZ RILEY

563. Famous military brats

AIR FORCE
Heloise Bowles, columnist
Rear Adm. Wendi B. Carpenter, U.S. Navy
John Cornyn, U.S. Senator
John Denver, singer
Mia Hamm, soccer player
Kris Kristofferson, singer/songwriter, actor
Annie Leibovitz, photographer
Priscilla Presley, actress
Victoria Principal, actress
Bart Starr, NFL Hall of Famer

ARMY
Hunter "Patch" Adams, doctor made famous by Robin Williams' film role
Christina Aguilera, singer
Jackson Browne, singer/songwriter
Faye Dunaway, actress
Newt Gingrich, politician
Sen. John Kerry, 2004 U.S. presidential candidate
Gen. Douglas MacArthur, Medal of Honor recipient and Supreme Allied Commander in the Pacific, WWII
Julianne Moore, actress
Shaquille O'Neal, basketball superstar
Lionel Richie, singer
Gen. H. Norman Schwarzkopf, commander of coalition forces in Desert Storm
Rachel Smith, Miss USA 2007

564. TroopTube

565. Birthrates that shoot up nine months after a redeployment for big units, seemingly resulting in a whole new generation like the "Baby Boomers"

Gore Vidal, novelist
Bruce Willis, actor
Reese Witherspoon, actress
Tiger Woods, professional golf champion

COAST GUARD

Thad Allen, retired U.S. Coast Guard admiral, Incident Commander, Federal Gulf of Mexico Oil Disaster Response

MARINES

Pat Conroy, bestselling author of *The Great Santini*
Emmylou Harris, singer
Robert Hays, actor
Heather Locklear, model and actress
Renee Montagne, National Public Radio news correspondent, cohost of *Morning Edition,* former cohost of *All Things Considered*
The Wilson Sisters, Ann and Nancy, of Heart, singer/songwriters

NAVY

Dennis C. Blair, retired U.S. Navy admiral
Bill Cosby, comedian and actor
Robert Duvall, actor
Kathie Lee Gifford, actress
Mark Hamill, actor
Adm. John S. McCain Jr., the late Commander in Chief, Pacific Command
Sen. John McCain, retired U.S. Navy captain, 2008 presidential candidate
Steve McQueen, actor
Jim Morrison, singer/songwriter

566. Scholarship programs

- National Military Family Association's Joanne Holbrook Patton Military Spouse Scholarships
- Fisher House Foundation's Scholarships for Military Children Program
- ThanksUSA's scholarship program for children and spouses

567. Showing pride and staying connected by wearing red, white, and blue pins, yellow ribbon pins, and deployment bracelets on a daily basis

During our son's first deployment to Afghanistan, he explained that each soldier wore an identification tag secured in the laces of one of his boots when they went out on a mission. When he returned from the mission, he removed it, punched a hole in the end without a hole and used 550 utility cord to fashion a bracelet. He then put the "bracelet" in an envelope with the dates and name of the mission. He sent it home to us. Eventually, many of our family members had a "deployment bracelet" from Darren to wear. When the bracelets were given to the individuals, there was still dirt from Afghanistan in the lettering. Wearing the bracelet was a conversation starter, "Oh, interesting bracelet you are wearing ..." It gave us an opportunity to remind others that we still have sons, daughters, fathers, mothers, brothers, sisters deployed in harm's way (whether military or civilian) ... and an opportunity to ask that they pray for them in their religious fashion.

–ROZ RILEY

568. Collecting cooking recipes from all over the world

569. Webcam conversations and kisses

570. Installation-wide yard sales

571. Stairwell living

572. The "fun" of checking off inventory numbers on moving day

573. Having incredible art made and framed for almost nothing in South Korea

574. Learning to love something about every duty station, even those "armpits" you are always warned about

Ironically, the places no one wants to go, among them Minot Air Force Base, North Dakota; Goodfellow Air Force Base, Texas; and Altus Air Force Base, Oklahoma, turn out to produce some of the best friends and the best memories.

–TERRI BARNES, Air Force spouse and *Spouse Calls* blog columnist

575. Looking out at stars at night as a way to connect to your loved one looking at the same stars across the globe

576. Reintegration

Understanding each other when dealing with the "honeymoon" or the "not-so-honeymoon" parts of reunion

577. Military brats connecting online
- **Military Brats Online** www.militarybratlife.com
- **Military Brats Registry** www.militarybrat.com
- **Military Teen Network** www.militaryteenonline.com

578. Feeling a connection every time you see a car with a DoD sticker

Especially in areas with few military—and always having the thought, "Wonder if we know them? We might!"

579. Being proactive about exploring your new town quickly, because you'll only be there a few years

I have to laugh at how often I introduced civilian neighbors to things they didn't know about their own town, even though they'd lived there for years (in some cases their whole lives). How is that possible? I think it's because I was always looking at the town with new eyes, curious to explore, to find out everything I could very quickly. But also it was because I always got lost a lot, especially in the years before GPS. Whereas my civilian friends tended to travel certain routes they'd been traveling for years, I'd be stumbling on all kinds of things as I got lost.

–KATHIE

580. Operation Footlocker, the mobile military brat footlocker monument

The American Overseas Schools Archives (AOSA) is dedicated to preserving the history and memorabilia (diaries, photographs, and stories) of an estimated four million American children who attended more than nine hundred American overseas schools over the past hundred and fifty years.

581. Truly appreciating what our military does when you tour the Korean Demilitarized Zone (DMZ)

582. GreenCare for Troops at www.projectevergreen.com/gcft
An outreach program helping to connect local professionals with military families in need of lawn care maintenance

583. Interactive Customer Evaluation (ICE)
The ICE system allows you to rate your experience and to offer comments on a wide range of activities and services on your specific installation. For better or for worse.

584. Tutor.com/military
Free tutoring for active-duty members and their families, 24/7

585. Freebies "because you're military"
Meals out, ball games, races, and more

For a list of Veterans Day freebies and discounts, see www.military.com/veterans-day/veterans-day-discounts.html

586. Mobile United Service Organizations' Center on Wheels

587. Unit and FRG fundraisers
Car washes, silent auctions, Christmas wrapping, bake sales, or first-kiss raffles

588. Abackpackjournalist.com
Internships in writing, video, and poetry for military children

589. Adoption subsidy
Reimburses specific adoption costs, including placement fees, legal fees, and medical expenses

590. Installation awards
From Installation Family of the Year Award and Installation Volunteer of the Year to Yard of the Month and others

591. Unit family newsletters and Facebook pages

592. Inexpensive golfing and great golf courses

- **Air Force Academy's Blue Course,** Colorado
- **Joint Base Andrews' South Course,** Maryland
- **Eglin Air Force Base's Eagle Course,** Florida
- **Joint Base Pearl Harbor-Hickam's courses,** Hawaii
- **Luke Air Force Base, Falcon Dunes,** Arizona
- **Vandenberg Air Force Base's Marshalia Ranch Golf Course,** California
- **Fort Ord's Bayonet Course,** California
- **Fort Benjamin Harrison's The Fort Golf Course,** Indiana
- **Joint Base Elmendorf-Richardson's courses,** Alaska
- **Joint Base Lewis-McChord's Golf Course,** Washington
- **Fort Sam Houston's Salado Del Rio Golf Course,** Texas
- **Fort Meade's Applewood Course,** Maryland
- **Fort Lee's The Cardinal Golf Club,** Virginia
- **Fort Jackson's Old Hickory Course,** South Carolina
- **Camp Pendleton Golf Course,** California
- **Kaneohe Klipper Golf Course,** Hawaii
- **The Legends at Parris Island,** South Carolina
- **Norfolk's Sewells Point Golf Course,** Virginia
- **Miramar Memorial Golf Course,** California
- **Naval Air Station Jacksonville's Golf Club,** Florida

List your favorite military golf courses

593. The many support programs available

At the installation Family Service Centers or through the Office of Work-Life Programs, especially deployment and mobilization support

I consider myself privileged to have served in the military, to be a veteran, and now to be a DoD civilian. I love being an Army Community Service Information and Referral program manager because I can assist families with gaining access to resources and services with those organizations that serve our military community. With this job, I feel as though I am honoring veterans, Service members, their families, and the military community all in one.

–CARLA MOSS, Army veteran and Army Community Service
Information and Referral program manager

594. Religious services that are often unique to the military

Singing "The Marine Hymn," "The Battle Hymn of the Republic," and "Amazing Grace" all in the same church service ...

–JOHN SCHAEFFER AND FRANK SCHAEFFER, *Keeping Faith*

595. Pear blossom cottages in South Korea

A place to make new friends and find out more about your new home and culture

596. Discounts for our service from restaurants to department stores to cruise ships

Many amusement parks—such as Disney and Anheuser-Busch theme parks, Sea World, Busch Gardens, and Sesame Place—offer military days that grant free admission or deeply discounted rates

597. Orientation programs

Like the People Encouraging People (PEP) welcome program in Germany, showing you the ropes of your new post and culture—and a great place to make new friends

598. Helpful information for parents of military

★ Vicki Cody's Guide, *Your Soldier Your Army*—a deployment survival guide for parents and spouses. Mrs. Cody turns her own thirty-year experience as the wife and mother of Soldiers into advice and consolation for other parents with deploying children. She covers the whole gamut, from the preparation through the endurance to the homecoming, and includes a personal view into Army life and an explanation of Army terminology.

Download your free copy by visiting www.ausa.org/publications/ilw/ilw_pubs/specialreports/documents/yoursoldier.pdf

★ Sandy Doell's book, *Mom's Field Guide*—a wonderful compilation of information relative to military parents. You can purchase a copy of this guide at her website, MomsFieldGuide.com. Sandy also has a support website at WhileOurChildrenserve.com.

★ *Keeping Faith: A Father-Son Story about Love and the U.S. Marine Corps* by John Schaeffer and Frank Schaeffer

★ *Minefields of the Heart: A Mother's Stories of a Son at War* by Sue Diaz

★ *Thriving Not Just Surviving: Deployment Perspectives for Today's Military Families* edited by Barbara Beyer

★ MarineParents.com—offering tons of support open to all Services, not just Marines

★ TodaysMilitary.com—for new or possible military parents wanting to find out more about the military before a son or daughter joins or before one leaves for boot camp

599. Walking up to the Seoul Tower

600. Military pets and their names ...

Sergeant, Sapper, Scout, Freedom, Artillery, Jody, Ranger ...

601. Gate guards, for keeping us safe and for bearing cold, wind, rain, and heat

CAKE IN  A JAR

Get wide-mouth canning jars. You can find them in housewares stores or online. Boil the jars to sterilize. Using a boxed cake mix or any cake recipe:

1. Make the cake batter according to the instructions or recipe.
2. Grease the jar by liberally spraying the inside with cooking spray.
3. Fill jar no more than halfway with batter.
4. Place jars on cookie sheet on rack in the oven. Bake at 400°F for 30-35 minutes or until a toothpick comes out clean.
5. While cake is baking, boil jar lids in a pan of water.
6. When cake is done, take one jar out at a time and cover with hot lid. Screw on jar ring, tightening it slightly.
7. The lid will seal as it cools. Listen to hear the "ping" as the lids seal.
8. As the cake cools, it will pull away from the jar slightly. That's OK; it just means that it will slide out of the jar easily.
9. Do not frost cake while in the jar! Send frosting along.
10. Make sure you wrap the jars well (bubble wrap is preferable, but wadded newspaper or clothing and other items will pad it too).

Remember to include a couple of plastic knives for the frosting and some plastic forks.

602. Sending your Service member a birthday greeting like "Cake in a Jar"

603. Operation Rising Star, the military's own American Idol road show

604. Unit family days

605. Shoppettes, your one stop to fill up and grab that "gallon of milk"

606. Defense Enrollment Eligibility Reporting System (DEERS)

If you're not "in" DEERS, you don't exist.

607. Making dinners for Fisher House families
Thankful you can do something to help and knowing that others will do the same for you should you ever need it

608. Mail Order Pharmacy at www.Express-Scripts.com
Refill prescriptions online, save up to 33 percent on cost, and swap driving to the pharmacy for free standard shipping.

609. Military chaplains
Charged with ensuring that their men and women are "spiritually fit to fight," they travel with, and face the same dangers as, their troops.

Photo by Staff Sgt. Samuel Morse

610. Operation Purple programs provided by National Military Family Association (NMFA)

★ **Operation Purple camps for military kids dealing with deployment:** Created in 2004 with an initial run of twelve camps serving one thousand military children, the mission of Purple Camp is to "empower military children and their families to develop and maintain healthy and connected relationships, in spite of the current military environment." The camps include a variety of activities tapping into the healing and holistic aspect of the natural world. In 2010, sixty-eight camps in thirty-seven states, as well as in Guam and Germany, provided programs for ten thousand military children.

★ **Operation Purple Healing Adventures:** Retreats for wounded Service members and their families

★ **Operation Purple Leadership Camp for teens:** Military teens build leadership skills and citizenship skills at these camps. As a requirement to attend this selective program, teens must complete a service project that benefits their community—from community clean-ups to starting deployment groups at their high school.

> *Each activity, designed to help us meet both our team and individual goals, forced us to work on our leadership and communication skills while bringing out abilities and talents we didn't even know we had. By the second day it was evident to the camp director how much we were connecting as a group. She was amazed watching us complete challenges most adults couldn't do. I believe we were able to form relationships easily because we had so much in common, being military teens and having a parent deployed. The camp was a lot of fun and the experience gave me the confidence and skills necessary to conquer . challenges I will face in the future.*

–MATTHEW CONSTANTINE,
Operation Purple Leadership Camp participant

★ **Operation Purple Family Retreat for families after deployment:** After positive response to the test program in 2009, the program expanded to ten family retreats in 2010. Held in National Parks all over the country, the retreats provide families with the opportunity to reconnect and make new memories as a family. Nearly a hundred and fifty families took part.

★ **NMFA also partners with the Army Wounded Warrior (AW2) Program:** Offering a weeklong Operation Purple day camp to the children of wounded warriors attending the annual AW2 Symposium.

611. Installation tree-lighting ceremonies during the holidays

612. GuidetoMilitaryTravel.com
Tips, checklists, giveaways, and reviews of some popular and off-the-beaten-path getaways

613. BuzzOffBase.com
A source for the most exciting events, fabulous restaurants, family entertainment, hottest nightlife, and best shopping around your military base

614. MilitaryAvenue.com
Supporting the relocation, travel, and lifestyle needs of the military family

615. Pawn shops, dry cleaners, and barber shops
The three things you know you'll find right outside the gate

616. Sunday brunch at the club

617. Phone trees

618. DeploymentKids.com

619. Boards in the children's classroom, locker room, or house of worship recognizing Service members whom they love

620. Identifying with other military parents

You Know You Are the Parent of Someone in the Military When ...

You have to ask your child to repeat themselves, next time "in English"

Your name is on a family care plan

You have flown cross-country to help out your daughter-in-law or son-in-law with the kids to ease the strains of involuntary "single parenthood"

Collect calls or calls at all hours of the night are welcomed, not admonished

You swell with pride when accompanied by your son or daughter in uniform or if someone asks what or how your child is doing these days

You Know You Are a Military Brat When ...

You are amazed at people who have never left their hometown

The question, "Where are you from?" has no simple answer, but it sure starts a conversation

You have had Thanksgiving or Christmas dinners in a Mess Hall or galley

You still have hospital corners on your bed

You've been put on KP or Mess duty in your own home

You've been "restricted to quarters" or put on "extra duty" as a kid

You got your first paying job during high school bagging groceries at the Commissary

Your parents tell you to "go police up your room" and you know what that means

621. Identifying with other military brats

You knew the rank and name of the kid next door's father before meeting the kid next door

You say "hooah" or "roger that" instead of saying "OK"

You categorize other kids as either fellow military brats or civilians

You fear turning twenty-one because you lose your military ID card

Your house had a building number rather than an address

The church you attended during childhood offered Protestant, Catholic, and Jewish services

You thought that PCS meant "pack your toys and say 'see ya later' to your friends"

You see a child crying as they say good-bye to their daddy as he goes off to combat, and you start crying because you know what that feels like

You referred to your sandbox as NTC

By the age of ten, you knew how to convert at least one foreign currency to U.S. dollars

You go to a grocery store and insist on calling it the Commissary

You have to explain that being born in Germany does not make you German

You have to tell your math teacher the last school was teaching subtraction, the new school was on division, and you missed multiplication

You thought vacations meant going stateside to visit the grandparents

You listened to Armed Forces and Voice of America radio for the first ten years of your life

You name schools in three countries on two continents when asked what high school you attended

You refer to your friends not only by name but by the state/country they live in

THE NATO STANDARD MILITARY ALPHABET

*Alpha Bravo Charlie Delta Echo Foxtrot Golf
Hotel India Juliet Kilo Lima Mike November
Oscar Papa Quebec Romeo Sierra Tango
Uniform Victor Whiskey X-ray Yankee Zulu*

ON THE INSIDE

JARGON

You know you are in the military—or connected to the military—when you immediately know what "last four," sponsor, double time, o-dark-thirty, and STRAC mean.

–KATHIE HIGHTOWER

622. The phonetic alphabet
The NATO standard military alphabet

623. Niner, tree, fife
Numbers nine, three, and five respectively
This way of saying numbers makes them easier to hear over a radio. Sometimes they are used in regular conversation or telephone conversation out of habit.

624. Measurements
Klick—kilometer
Mike Mike—millimeter
Mikes—minutes

625. Mosquito wings/butterfly stripes/dragonfly wings
Those junior promotions and the ribbing that goes with them

626. Barracks rat
A person who is unwilling or unable to go "out in town" during liberty

627. Lance Corporal Underground
A Marine term for the junior enlisted rumor mill

628. Skivvies and civvies

629. Lackland Lasers
GI flashlights with about a six-inch light-saber–like attachment, carried by basic trainees at Lackland Air Force Base, Texas (home of Air Force recruit training)

630. Birth Control Glasses (BCGs), aka GI glasses
Handed out to Armed Forces recruits at recruit training, where contact lenses and civilian eyeglasses are strictly prohibited. The glasses are designed with the emphasis on maximum durability at minimum cost. Made of brown plastic, GI glasses are impact-resistant, waterproof, and, shall we say, not very becoming. Reflecting this last point is their nickname—BCGs, or Birth Control Glasses.

631. Newbies

MORE NAMES FOR NEW RECRUITS

- Blue head
- Boot or booter
- Butter bar or Jeff if you're Air Force
- Croot or cruit
- Grunt
- Nonusable body (NUB)
- Nugget
- Ping
- Ricky
- SMACK—Soldier minus ability, coordination, and knowledge
- Smurf
- Worm

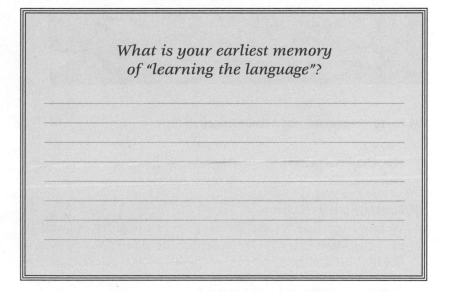

*What is your earliest memory
of "learning the language"?*

632. Basic training-ese

★ Method behind the madness

★ The "right" way (the recruit way) versus the "wrong" way (the nasty civilian way)

★ Break you down in order to build you up again

★ **Double time**—A quick or running pace. Recruits must "double time" if they are not marching with their unit.

★ **Walking chit**—A permission slip so the recruit may walk, not run, to their destination when not in ranks

★ **Ricky carwash**—Short shower that the recruits take

★ **Ricky lawnmower**—Nail clippers, used to trim stray threads from uniforms

★ **Ricky rocket/go-go juice**—A boot camp "energy drink" made from an assorted mix of sodas, sports drinks, coffee, sugar, and artificial sweeteners, used to help keep the recruit awake

★ **"It's a rifle**—your weapon, Private—not a gun."

You Know You Are a Service Member When ...

Your child's first words were "Good to Go, Sir"

633. Heard, Understood, and Acknowledged (HUA)

Hooah!	Oorah!
Yes, Drill Sergeant!	Roger.
Aye, Aye, Sir!	Sir, yes SIR!

634. Company-grade weather

Weather too bad for the senior pilots to venture out and fly in. They leave it for the company-grade pilots. As opposed to field-grade weather.

635. Wannabes—always good for a chuckle

636. Crawling out of the rack

637. Plank owner—something like a "charter member"

A plank owner is a crew member who has been with a ship since its commissioning.

638. Fun hazing

MILITARY PRACTICAL JOKES

- Canopy lights
- Chem light batteries
- Echo check
- Flight line
- Grid squares
- ID10T Forms
- Keys to the aircraft/ submarine/ship
- Pad eye cleaner
- Checking for soft spots on a vehicle
- PRC-E7s

639. Terms of endearment for other specialties or Services

AIR FORCE
Chair Force
Fly Bears
Zoomies
Blue Suiters
Bus Driver

ARMY
Dogface or Doggies
Ground Pounder
Joe
Green Suiters

COAST GUARD
Coastie
Shipmate
Guardian

MARINES
Devil Dog
Jarhead
Leatherneck

NAVY
Bubble Heads
Squids
Swabbies
Sand Crabs

As we write this, we wonder how the latest Army uniform change will affect the long-held nickname "Green Suiter." Now that Class As are blue rather than green, will the old nickname hold? After all, if it changes to Blue Suiter, how will we distinguish the Army from the Air Force?

A joint assignment makes you a Purple Suiter—purple is the military symbol for "joint," meaning all Services. Why? If you combine the colors of Air Force blue, Army green, Coast Guard blue, Marine Corps red, and Navy blue, you get the color purple.

640. Bravo Zulu
Coast Guard and Navy's "well done"

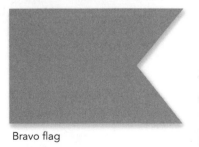

Bravo flag

Zulu flag

>> **DID YOU KNOW?**

Many of us in the military use the term STRAC all the time. We know what it means but how many of us know where it came from? It was the acronym and motto of the Strategic Army Corps, a command of the U.S. Army in the 1960s. "Skilled, Tough, Ready Around the Clock," for its mission of being ready at a moment's notice.

641. The picture of efficiency

High-speed, low drag	Super slick
Teflon coated	Lean and mean
Squared away	Shipshape
STRAC	

642. The many ways to get attention and make ready

Now hear this!	All hands on deck!
Make a hole!	Gangway!
On the double!	Take a knee!
Stand by!	Anchors aweigh!
Pull chocks!	

"Hurry up and wait"

643. Jane Wayne—especially Hooah! females

644. Smokey Bear

Apt name for military instructors because of the round brown hat they wear while serving as drill sergeants or training instructors

645. Secret Squirrel

A nickname for Military Intelligence or Special Operations. We can't tell you more. As the saying goes, "If we told you, we'd have to kill you."

646. Angles and dangles

Diving deep and resurfacing steeply in a submarine—a way to check for loose items and noisemakers before continuing out to sea

Petty Officer 3rd Class Erika Rice, yeoman, and other Sailors man the rails of USS *Abraham Lincoln*.

Photo by Petty Officer 2nd Class James Evans

647. Forming up

Fall in!

Ah-ten-hut!

Dress Right Dress!

Man the rails!

648. "Marine Thunder"

> ... *the "crack!-crunch!-crack!" of eighty heels*
> *striking the parade deck as one in perfect harmony*

–JOHN SCHAEFFER AND FRANK SCHAEFFER, *Keeping Faith*

649. O-beer-thirty

Time of dismissal from the day's duties, time for a beer, also close of business (COB). Don't forget to "pop smoke"!

650. Dog and pony shows

Also known as canine and equestrian theater
"Get ready for the VIP!"

651. Humps
Road marches or ruck marches while in full combat gear with heavy rucks

652. Nicknames or terms of endearment for a couple of Service academies
Zoomie U—what the Marines call the U.S. Air Force Academy, but they really are the Fighting Falcons
Canoe U—U.S. Naval Academy nickname, unofficially

653. Hatch
A door. Many bring the shipboard terminology to land, saying, "shut the hatch," which really just means "door."

654. In theater
Nothing to do with going to the movies, but means being deployed or "in country"

655. Digit
Navy term for butterfly-folding multitool such as a Leatherman or Gerber

656. Ma Deuce
A .50-caliber machine gun (M2)

657. Pea shooter
Not an M2, but something much smaller

658. "Ready on the right? Ready on the left? Ready on the firing line? Commence firing ..."

659. Pogey bait and gedunk

660. Cover—as in, protect

661. All the nicknames for uniforms or uniform items

Fruit Salad	Service Charlies (Marines)
Digi-man or Digies	Bird Colonel or Full Bird
Chest Candy	Scrambled eggs (the golden leaf
Cammies	embellishments on dress hats)

662. "People tanks," a play off of fish tank

Used by Navy and refers to a submarine with personnel inside

663. Hootch—home away from home

Originally used in Vietnam as a term for a thatch hut, it now refers to a simple dwelling or your "personal space" when deployed.

664. Battle rattle

Imagine yourself walking along with helmet, ruck, weapon, mask, ammo pouches, and so forth—that is, "in full battle rattle." Clunk-clunk-rattle-rattle!

665. LN

Local national or "friendly"

666. LPCs

Leather personnel carriers, aka boots

667. Snivel gear

668. Ranger coffee

From an MRE, instant coffee straight from the packet

669. Ranger pudding

From an MRE, combine cocoa mix, sugar, instant coffee, instant creamer, and water for the desired consistency.

670. Ranger candy

Pain relievers or any other cure-all

671. Beans and bullets

672. Bean counters to count the beans and bullets

673. O-dark-thirty

Sometime after midnight but before a "normal" formation time. One either stays up until o-dark-thirty to complete the mission or gets up at o-dark-thirty to start an early duty day.

674. Fall out! or Dismissed!

Sometimes it feels as if sweeter words have never been heard.

675. Short

Quickly approaching the end of one's service, usually comes with attitude

676. Cover—as in, headgear

Patrol caps, berets, or helmets—never a "hat"!

677. Your "six"

Buddies who cover your "six" have "got your back."

678. Target-rich environment

679. Putting kiwi on boots

This does not involve fruit.

680. Hookers

Kiddie name for blousing bands

681. Hardball

Any hard-surfaced road

682. Tango Mike

"Thanks much"

683. Over and Out

The last word—what slang or jargon would your military life not be the same without?

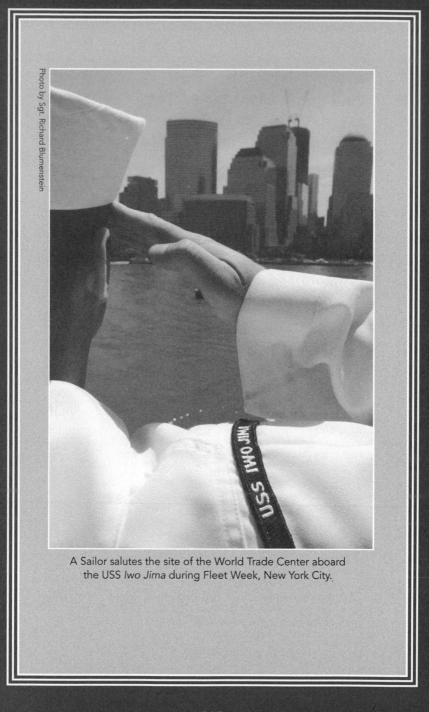

A Sailor salutes the site of the World Trade Center aboard the USS *Iwo Jima* during Fleet Week, New York City.

ON THE INSIDE

TRADITIONS

A way to see our pride of service is through military customs, courtesies, and traditions. These are what connect us with those who have traveled this military journey before us.

–HOLLY SCHERER

684. Retreat and To the Colors
Pausing and facing toward the nearest flag at the end of a day

685. Learning customs and courtesies that will be applicable for a lifetime

686. A salute
A sign of honor and respect

687. Honoring the flag

> *For your country, boy, and for your flag, never dream a dream but of serving her as she bids you, though the service carry you through a thousand hells. No matter what happens to you, no matter who flatters you or who abuses you, never look at another flag, never let a night pass but you pray God to bless that flag.*

–EDWARD EVERETT HALE, "The Man Without a Country"

688. Jody calls or cadences

The camaraderie and inspiration taking your mind off the exertion and effort of running or marching

Working hard for Uncle Sam,
Ready to fight for my fellow man

THEY SAY THAT IN THE ARMY

They say that in the Army the coffee's mighty fine
it looks like muddy water and tastes like turpentine

Chorus
Oh Lord, I wanna go
But they won't let me go
Oh Lord, I wanna go hoo-hoo-hoooome EH!

Additional Verses
They say that in the Army ...

... the chow is mighty fine
a chicken jumped off the table and started marking time

... the biscuits are mighty fine
one rolled off the table and killed a friend of mine

... the training's mighty fine
last night there were ten of us, now there's only nine

... the pay is mighty fine
they give you a hundred dollars and take back ninety-nine

☆

OLD KING COLE

Old King Cole was a merry old soul
and a merry old soul was he, uh huh.
He called for his pipe, and he called for his bowl
and he called for his privates three, uh huh.
Beer! Beer! Beer! cried the privates.
Brave men are we
There's none so fair as they can compare
to the airborne infantry, uh huh.

Old King Cole was a merry old soul
and a merry old soul was he
He called for his pipe and he called for his bowl
and he called for his corporals three
I need a three-day pass said the corporals
Beer, beer, beer said the privates
Merry men are we
But none so fair that they can compare
to the airborne infantry

Additional Verses

Sergeants three—"File from the left, column right said the Sgts"

Looeys three—"I'll lead the way said the looeys"

Captains three—"Charge that hill said the captains"

Majors three—"Who's gonna shine my boots said the majors"

Colonels three—"Where's my star said the colonels"

Generals three—"War, War, War said the generals"

☆

EVERYWHERE WE GO

Everywhere we go-o
People wanna know-o
Who we are
So we tell them
We're not the Army
The backpackin' Army
We're not the Air Force
The low flyin' Air Force
We're not the Mo-rines
They don't even look mean
We're not the Coast Guard
They don't even work hard
We are the Navy
The world's greatest Navy
The mighty-mighty Navy

★

MARINE INFANTRY

Hey there Army, get in your tanks and follow me,
I am Marine Corps infantry.
Hey there Air Force, get in your planes and follow me,
I am Marine Corps infantry.
Hey there Navy, get in your ships and follow me,
I am Marine Corps infantry.

AMERICAN WAY

Working hard for Uncle Sam,
Ready to fight for my fellow man.
Freedom, freedom, that's what I say,
Fighting for the American way.
Forever we hold our banner high,
We'll hold it up forever until we die.
Winning wars is what we do,
Fighting hard for me and you.
We will take them by the sky,
Beatin' the hell outta the other guy.
U.S. Air Force will make you pay,
Fighting for the American way.

★

Hey there JARHEADS, grab your M16 and follow me,
we are the Marine Corps infantry.
Hey there recon, grab your Ka-Bar and follow me,
you are the best of the infantry.
Hey civilians, get off your butts and sign up now,
join the Marine Corps infantry.

★

689. Reveille and other bugle calls

Adjutant's Call, Boots and Saddles, Charge!, and Taps

CANCEL REVEILLE? HORRORS!

In May 2010, the commander of Ellsworth Air Force Base, South Dakota, decided to cancel the 6:30 a.m. bugle calls. Why? Because he'd been getting complaints that the music was waking up children. After checking the Air Force regulations, he found no guidance requiring Reveille be played.

The response from the community was immediate. One anonymous person wrote into the base website, "That's like saying 'do not fly bombers at night because someone might be kept awake.' "

Within weeks the commander reversed his decision.

On his Facebook page, he wrote: "After discussing with some of the other senior officers under my command, it's clear the not playing of reveille has touched a nerve with our airmen and their families that has become a distraction to the mission." He did, however, move the bugle playing from 6:30 to 7:30 a.m.

Military tradition rules the day.

690. Ruffles (on the drums) and flourishes (by bugle or band)

691. Dining-Ins/Dining-Outs/Mess Nights

692. Mess dress or dinner dress

693. Receiving lines

694. Flyovers

695. Gun salutes

696. "Piped over the side"

697. Posting and retiring the Colors

Photo by Master Sgt. Brian Boisvert

Airmen from the 97th Air Mobility Wing raising the flag at Wings of Freedom Park, Altus Air Force Base, Okla.

>>> **DID YOU KNOW?** >

A retired U.S. Marine, Charles Tobias, rescued the British Royal Navy rum recipe and opened a distillery in Tortola, British Virgin Islands. He partnered with the Man Company to establish Pusser's Limited. The closely guarded naval recipe is still used at Pusser's today.

1775 RUM PUNCH
1 part lime juice
2 parts sugar syrup
3 parts dark rum (preferably Pusser's)
4 parts water

Mix, pour over ice, or chill. Top with a sprinkle of nutmeg and dash of Angostura bitters. May substitute pineapple juice for water.

HOT GROG
1 shot rum (preferably Pusser's)
1 teaspoon sugar
Squeeze of lime
Cinnamon stick
Boiling water

Stir ingredients; add enough boiling water to fill mug.

698. The long-lived tradition of a rum toast—also known as "The Grog"

699. Military balls—and their established traditions
- **Wine toast**—Decanter passed from left to right around the table, never stopping until the glasses are "charged." Raising your glasses and remembering all whom we respect and honor from the President of the United States to our country, to our fallen comrades, to the ladies at the ball.
- **Punch bowl ceremony**—Called by some units "The Grog." Usually prepared using specific ingredients that represent the many battles and campaigns of the unit/squadron/ regiment/division. Each ingredient represents those who have gone before and the commitment and responsibility to continue to serve. Examples: Cold War—Russian vodka;

Invasion of France—champagne; Korean War—Soju; Gulf War—crude oil (maple syrup); Fallen Comrades—sand (brown sugar). Only lack of creativity hinders the type of ingredients used.

- **The lone and empty table complete with place setting—** representing the Service member who is not able to be present because he or she is deployed, is POW/MIA, or paid the ultimate sacrifice. We will always remember!
- **Marine Corps cake-cutting ceremony—**By tradition, the first pieces of cake go to three people: one to the ball's guest of honor, the next to the oldest Marine at the ball, and the third piece to the youngest Marine in attendance. It's a solemn moment symbolizing the old passing the traditions and the love of the Corps to the new.
- **Swag—**promotional items, "take-aways," at the ball. It could be anything from local wine with the unit's label on the front to wine glasses with the unit's crest to unit memorabilia.

Photo by Staff Sgt. April Melton

Adding special ingredients to "The Grog"

700. New military ball traditions—especially since the beginning of the wars in Iraq and Afghanistan

One thing that sets our military life apart from that of our non-military peers is the frequent opportunity to participate in long-standing traditions, often hundreds of years old. The pageantry of a military ball is one tradition that members of all services experience. But what happens when circumstances change for some members of our community?

In 2005, Marine spouse Lynne Crowe noticed that for many spouses the experience of the Marine Corps Birthday Ball had changed. When a military member is deployed, a spouse attending on her own can feel awkward. Yet not attending means missing out on this rich annual esprit-building event. Feelings of aloneness stand out either way.

Lynne decided to tweak this annual tradition in a way to honor the new circumstances. With the help of the community and other spouses at Twentynine Palms Marine Corps Base, California, she created a ball for spouses of deployed Marines. To add an extra element of fun, the event became the Ugly Gown Ball. Sixty spouses showed up for dinner, dancing, and a chance to win the prize for the ugliest gown. (Talk about a different experience in getting ready for a military ball when we are all usually trying our hardest to look our best!)

Family Readiness Groups of deployed units have hosted "mock Dining-Ins" for the same reason. Just as traditional military unit Dining-Ins foster camaraderie and esprit de corps, the "mock Dining-In" does the same for family members during long deployments. Groups of spouses compete to have the best skit and table decorations according to themes that honor their unit's military affiliation and history.

The 2006 Ugly Gown Ball at Twentynine Palms was open to all Marine Corps spouses whether a spouse was deployed or not. Anne Woods, who helped to coordinate that year's event, said, "This is a way to continue to honor the Marine Corps traditions, as well as a way for military spouses to strengthen their bonds of friendship." More than one hundred spouses showed up for the 2006 event.

Instead of the tradition of the oldest and youngest Marine cutting the cake, the longest and newest married spouse cut the cake. Prizes for the ugliest gowns of the '60s, '70s, and '80s, in addition to the runner-up and grand prize winners, prompted many attendees to say, "We can't wait to start looking for our ugliest gowns for next year's ball." Looks like a new military tradition has been born.

701. Service ribbons

702. Medals

703. Unit heraldry—symbols of a unit's history, mission, or function

Guidons, streamers, decorations, and coats of arms for identification and esprit de corps

Photo by Sgt. 1st Class Kevin Doheny

The guidon of Forward Support Company, 2nd Battalion, 320th Field Artillery Regiment, blows in the wind in Iraq.

704. Awards for military service

705. Change of Command ceremonies
Passing the organizational flag

706. Marines' 8th and I Evening Parade
An unforgettable experience!

707. Drill and ceremonies
Dress Right, DRESS; Forward, MARCH; About, FACE

708. Promotion ceremonies

709. Promotion parties and Wetting Down parties

710. "Sabering" a champagne bottle with a military sword to celebrate any special event

711. Military graduations

712. Retirement ceremonies and speeches

713. Parade fields and parade decks

714. Honor Guard

715. Inspections

716. Cresting ceremony

717. Frocking or pinning ceremony

718. Reenlistment ceremonies

> *Unlike the draftees of the Civil War or even the
> Greatest Generation of World War II, these soldiers
> do not become farmers or businessmen or schoolteachers
> when their tour is over. They reenlist. They are proud,
> lean, and hard. If they have families, their wives and
> children are battered but tough. The soldiers of this
> generation are arguably the best fighters in the world.*
>
> –DAVID BOWNE WOOD, "In the 10th Year of War, a Harder Army,
> a More Distant America," Politics Daily, Sept. 9, 2010

719. "Fini" flights
A pilot's final flight and the fun of dousing the pilot with water before toasting with champagne

720. Right Arm Night or Boss's Night

Leaders come together with those standing to their right—the ones helping them get through daily missions—to build relationships while mixing and mingling with other leaders who have brought their battle buddies with them.

721. Enlisted/NCO/Officer/Community Clubs

A military tradition promoting camaraderie and esprit de corps

722. Field day

723. Line-crossing ceremony

In a centuries-old seafaring tradition, this Navy rite of passage baptizes any passengers or crew making their first crossing of the equator. Among similar traditions celebrating other significant crossings are rites to initiate sailors into the Orders of the Blue Nose, the Ditch, and the Magellan—for crossing the Arctic Circle, passing through the Panama Canal, and circumnavigating the globe, respectively.

Photo by Petty Officer 2nd Class James Evans

Sailors aboard USS *Carl Vinson* participate in a Crossing the Line Ceremony to mark the ship's passage over the equator.

724. Marine Corps Marathon
Start: Arlington National Cemetery
Finish: Marine Corps War Memorial

What other marathon lets you draw inspiration from all the important monuments in the Nation's Capital, including memorials to FDR, Lincoln, and Jefferson, the National World War II Memorial, Korean War Veterans Memorial, and Vietnam Veterans Memorial, as well as the Washington Monument, the U.S. Capitol, and all the museums on the National Mall? No wonder this 26.2-mile race is nicknamed "The Marathon of the Monuments."

725. Army Ten Miler
Start: Arlington National Cemetery
Finish: Pentagon

In the course of this historic race, runners pass the Lincoln Memorial, Kennedy Center, Washington Monument, National World War II Memorial, Korean War Veterans Memorial, District of Columbia War Memorial, Smithsonian Institution, American History Museum, Natural History Museum, U.S. Capitol, National Museum of the American Indian, Air and Space Museum, Hirshhorn Museum, and Holocaust Museum.

726. Navy Five Miler and the new Navy Ten Nautical Miler

727. Air Force Winterfest

728. Coast Guard Fest
Saluting Coasties and the mission they love

729. Shadow runs
Thousands of miles from home, military members take part in road racing. "Shadow runs" allow them to participate in some of the States' most popular events, such as the Army Ten Miler and the Boston Marathon—only service members run them while deployed overseas, complete with banners, chip timing, and finishers' T-shirts.

Photo by Spc. Devin Kornaus

The Fife and Drum Corps, 3rd U.S. Infantry Regiment (The Old Guard), performs during Twilight Tattoo at Fort Lesley J. McNair, Washington, D.C.

730. Tattoo—a thrill to experience!

tattoo (noun; pl. tattoos) 1. an evening drum or bugle signal recalling soldiers to their quarters. 2. a military display consisting of music, marching, and exercises.

The term dates from the seventeenth century when the British Army was fighting in the Low Countries (Belgium and the Netherlands). Drummers from the garrison were sent out into the towns at 2130 each evening to inform the soldiers that it was time to return to barracks. The process was known as "doe den tap toe" and encouraged the innkeepers to turn off the taps, stop serving beer, and send the soldiers home for the night. The drummers continued to play until the curfew at 2200.

731. All-Hands events
- All-Hands Call
- All-Hands parties
- Coast Guard's All-Hands Picnic

732. Installation Oktoberfest celebrations

733. Devil Dogs and Devil Dog runs

734. Ceremonies in the life of a ship
- **Keel laying**—In this ceremony at the shipyard, the keel is placed in the cradle where the ship will be built.

- **Christening or launching**—In this ceremony, also conducted by the shipbuilder, a new vessel is given her name and committed to sea.

- **Commissioning**—In this ceremony, a vessel officially becomes a United States Ship (USS) or U.S. Coast Guard (USCG) vessel when the commissioning pennant is broken at the masthead. With this act, the ship becomes a Navy or Coast Guard command in her own right and takes her place alongside the other active ships of the Fleet.

- **Decommissioning**—This ceremony officially ends a ship's active duty.

735. Battle saints
- St. Barbara
- St. Anthony of Padua
- St. John of Capistrano
- Joan of Arc
- Gabriel, the Archangel
- St. George
- St. Michael
- St. Martin
- St. Philip Neri
- St. Joseph of Cupertino
- St. Sebastian

Photo by Capt. Samuel Perez

U.S. naval ships moored at Mina Salman Pier, Bahrain, hoist flags and pennants for Dress Ship as part of a Fourth of July celebration.

736. Dressing Ship and Holiday Colors
Definitely a beautiful photo opportunity!

737. Military Service birthdays

GOOD REASONS TO CELEBRATE!

Navy's Submarine Force birthday	April 11
Army Reserves birthday	April 23
Army birthday	June 14
Coast Guard birthday	August 4
Air Force birthday	September 18
Navy birthday	October 13
Marines birthday	November 10
National Guard birthday	December 13

>> **DID YOU KNOW?**

There has been a Sentinel on duty in front of the Tomb of the Unknown Soldier in Arlington National Cemetery every minute of every day since 1937. Even during Hurricane Isabel in 2003, sentries guarding the tomb remained at their posts.

738. Tomb of the Unknown Soldier

739. Cemeteries here and abroad dedicated to American Service members

You can't help but feel a sense of awe and connection as you walk through Arlington National Cemetery or any of the American cemeteries overseas.

740. Oral histories

Efforts by veterans, military family members, and others to capture the stories of military life over the ages. Two examples:

The Veterans History Project of the American Folklife Center at the Library of Congress

This project collects, preserves, and makes accessible personal accounts of American war veterans so that future generations can hear directly from veterans to better understand the realities of war. The project includes firsthand accounts of U.S. veterans from World War I through Operation New Dawn in Iraq and Operation Enduring Freedom in Afghanistan.

The U.S. Congress created the Veterans History Project in 2000, and it's made possible by the generous support of Congress. See more at www.loc.gov/vets/about.html.

The Army Family Oral History Project

In 1989, after the fall of the Berlin Wall and the reunification of Germany, the United States began to withdraw units that had been stationed in West Germany since the end of World War II. Many of the units not only left Germany, they also left the active-duty rolls.

Memorabilia such as unit colors and battle streamers, unit histories, photos, and trophies of each of the deactivated units were sent back to the States and stored until such time as the unit would be reactivated.

What was not authorized to be shipped back and stored were items that pertained to the wives' activities over that same period of time. This oversight made two spouses realize that all too often descriptions and details of family activities and experiences are not recorded anywhere and are therefore lost. Mary Ann Meigs and Betty Rutherford decided to find a way to capture at least some of the Army's distaff experiences.

In 1998, the Army Family Oral History Project began under the auspices of the History Office of the Combined Arms Center at Fort Leavenworth, Kansas. Most of the work is done by dedicated volunteers. The goal of the project is to interview a broad range of Army wives, starting with the oldest, recording memories, stories, and experiences they had while their husbands were on active duty.

The transcribed, edited, and indexed interviews are stored in the Special Collections Archives of the Combined Arms Research Library at Fort Leavenworth, available to interested historians and other researchers.

741. Great books of letters written by Service members
War Letters and *Grace under Fire* were both edited by Andrew Carroll, whose "Legacy Project" is aimed at preserving wartime correspondence.

Visit the website at www.warletters.com.

742. Fleet Week
Being able to board ships/vessels belonging to the U.S. Navy, U.S. Marine Corps, and U.S. Coast Guard and seeing life aboard the ship

743. Plebes and doolies

744. Tanks

An F-15C receives fuel from the boom of a KC-135 Stratotanker.

745. Military planes/jets
Transporter, fighter, bomber, airlifter, passenger, intelligence, surveillance, recon, and so many more

746. Humvees

747. Submarines

748. Ships
Battleships, aircraft carriers, cruisers, destroyers—not *boats*

749. Tactical vehicles
Security, fighting, and unmanned aerial ones too

Photo by Petty Officer 2nd Class Brooks B. Patton Jr.

An HH-60H Sea Hawk helicopter flies in front of the aircraft carrier USS *Enterprise* as it transits the Strait of Bab el Mandeb.

750. Helicopters, aka helos or choppers

Black Hawks, Whitehawks, Jayhawks, Seahawks, Pave Hawks, Chinooks, Vipers, Iroquois ... and the list goes on. Each service has its helicopters ... different models, different names, different missions

751. Military colleges

- The Citadel
- North Georgia College and State University
- Norwich University
- Mary Baldwin Women's Institute for Leadership
- Texas A&M University
- The Virginia Military Institute (VMI)
- Virginia Polytechnic Institute and State University (Virginia Tech)

752. Class rings

Many times, class rings are worn next to wedding bands. At the Naval Academy, the rings are blessed during the Ring Dance.

753. Cadets

> *The mothers and fathers of America will give you their sons and daughters ... with the confidence in you that you will not needlessly waste their lives. And you dare not. That's the burden the mantle of leadership places upon you. You could be the person who gives the orders that will bring about the deaths of thousands and thousands of young men and women. It is an awesome responsibility. You cannot fail. You dare not fail.*

–GEN. H. NORMAN SCHWARZKOPF, from a speech to West Point Cadets in May 1991

754. Military academies

- U.S. Air Force Academy
- U.S. Coast Guard Academy
- West Point, the U.S. Military Academy
- U.S. Naval Academy

Photo by Petty Officer 2nd Class Chad Runge

Newly commissioned officers toss their covers during the U.S. Naval Academy Class of 2011 graduation and commissioning ceremony.

755. Military bands

*Stated hours to be assigned, for all the drums and fifes,
of each regiment, to attend them and practice—Nothing
is more agreeable, and ornamental, than good music;
every officer, for the credit of his corps, should take care
to provide it.*

–GEORGE WASHINGTON

Military bands have been included in the ranks since the Continental Army of 1776 to provide music to sustain warrior morale, foster military pride, inspire leaders, build good will with the local populace, and serve at ceremonies such as parades, presidential inaugurations, and military funerals.

Military bands are assigned to specific military bases or units and are associated with each of the service academies. Across the services, ten bands are considered to be premier. Members of these bands often come from prestigious conservatories and schools of music.

In all services, other bands are staffed with members who have enlisted in their applicable branch of service, completed basic training alongside other enlistees, and then competed in an audition to attend one of the Armed Forces' music schools. Once inducted, band members are assigned to a designated installation to provide musical support, but also understand that they are warriors first when they find themselves in a combat zone. Today's military bands are rewriting their "field manuals" and organizing smaller, more deployable groups in order to reach Service members deployed in remote areas.

The Air Force Bands Program, established in 1941, has twelve active-duty Air Force bands and eleven Air National Guard bands as well as the renowned Air Force Academy Band. Within the U.S. Air Force Band there are six performing ensembles: Concert Band, Singing Sergeants, Airmen of Note, Air Force Strings, Ceremonial Brass, and Max Impact.

As the largest branch of the Armed Forces, the U.S. Army has four premier bands and thirty traditional bands. There are also

Reserve and National Guard bands. The United States Army Band "Pershing's Own" has led every inaugural parade since 1925. The Army Field Band members are the musical ambassadors of the Army; they have four components: Concert Band, Soldiers' Chorus, Jazz Ambassadors, and The Volunteers. Each travels more than 100 days annually. Other large bands such as the Old Guard Fife and Drum Corps and the West Point Academy Band continue to be in the spotlight for their excellence.

The United States Coast Guard Band became the permanent, official musical representative of the nation's oldest continuous seagoing service in 1965. Originally a small command band located at the Coast Guard Academy and used primarily for local purposes, the band today routinely tours throughout the United States and overseas.

The United States Marine Band "The President's Own" was established in 1798 by an Act of Congress. This band is the oldest professional musical organization in the United States. It is well known for its public performances (about 500 per year across the United States) and performances at the White House and Inauguration Day festivities. In addition to "The President's Own," there are twelve other active-duty Marine Corps bands.

The United States Navy Band program has two premier bands—the United States Navy Band and the Naval Academy Band—and eleven active-duty fleet bands. Established in 1925, the U.S. Navy Band is composed of a concert-ceremonial unit and four specialty units: the Sea Chanters choir, The Commodores jazz ensemble, the Country Current group, and the Cruisers contemporary music ensemble.

DID YOU KNOW?

The Fightin' Texas Aggie Band of Texas A&M University is composed entirely of ROTC cadets and is the world's largest military marching band.

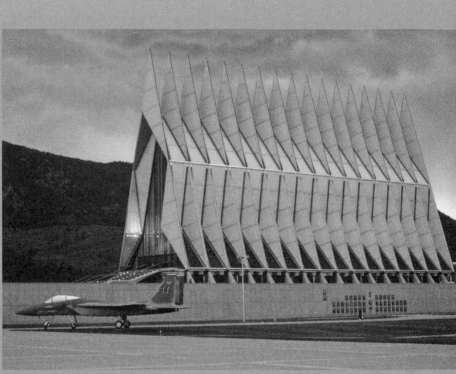

The U.S. Air Force Academy's Cadet Chapel is the most popular man-made attraction in Colorado, with more than a half million visitors every year.

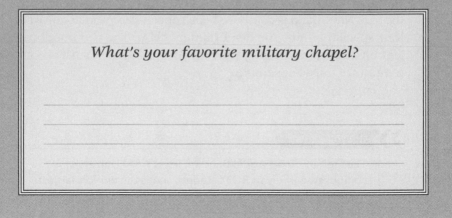

What's your favorite military chapel?

756. Historic military wedding chapels

Because of their picturesque settings, military chapels and academies often host military weddings. All Service academies have more than one chapel; at the Air Force Academy, for example, there are Protestant, Catholic, and Jewish chapels.

Each military installation also has its own chapel or chapels, each with its own beauty.

PICTURE-PERFECT VENUES NOTED BY FRIENDS

Air Force Academy Chapel, Colorado

Buckley Air Force Base Chapel, Colorado

Randolph Air Force Base Chapel, Texas

Fort Bragg Main Post Chapel, North Carolina

Joint Base Myer-Henderson Hall Chapel, Virginia

U.S. Coast Guard Memorial Chapel, Connecticut

Marine Corps Museum Chapel, Virginia

Pensacola Naval Air Station Chapel, Florida

Corpus Christi Naval Air Station Chapel, Texas

757. Former military chapels that have been restored

MORE BEAUTIFUL WEDDING VENUES

Fort Snelling Memorial Chapel, Minnesota

Presidio Chapel, California

Fort Mason Mission Chapel, California

Eisenhower Chapel, Colorado

The Chapel at Camp Colton, Oregon

Photo by Capt. Angela Webb

758. Sabers

759. Military weddings "Under the Sabers"—what could be more romantic?

Military weddings are a privilege of cadets or those in the Armed Forces. Often performed in military chapels, the traditions may also be transferred to civilian churches. Military members in the wedding party and many guests wear dress uniforms—but what most guests remember is the "crossed sabers." Also known as the "arch of sabers" or the "arch of steel," these are the sabers for Navy or swords for Army, Air Force, and Marines. Traditionally the bride and groom walk beneath the arch, a passage meant to ensure the couple's safe transition into their new life together.

The arch of swords is formed by an honor guard made up of members of the military standing in two lines opposite each other. At the command "draw sword" or "draw sabers," the steel is raised with the right hand, with the cutting edge facing up. The married couple enters the arch at the head of the line and walks to the end. Here traditions vary, but the couple will often be stopped by the lowering of the final two sabers in a demand that they kiss. A Marine Corps tradition, often adopted by the other services, is for the last saber bearer to "tap" the bride on the back of her dress with his saber and say, "Welcome to the Marine Corps, Ma'am." At the reception, tradition calls for the wedding cake to be cut with a saber or other type of military sword.

Some couples opt for horse-drawn carriages reminiscent of older times in the military, but others vary that tradition as well: "Gordon and I rode on a M24 Chaffee Tank from the chapel to our reception at the battalion dining facility!" says Linda Thompson, a retired Army lieutenant colonel. Janet McIntosh and her husband Dan, both motor transport drivers, were actually married on a HET (Heavy Equipment Transporter Vehicle), surrounded by a semi-circle of ten other HETS, with their drivers honking their horns and cheering. "Not the wedding I dreamed of since I was a little girl," says Janet, "but definitely a creative and memorable wedding day for my soldier and me."

760. Laughing when watching the movie *The Renaissance Man* with Danny DeVito as he asks for directions on a military base, is bombarded with acronyms, and finally asks, "Can I buy a vowel?"

761. Protocol

762. Armories

763. Hangars

764. The Pentagon

765. Armed Forces Network Radio in Europe and Korea (AFN)

766. Acronyms
Absolutely no one can do acronyms like the military.

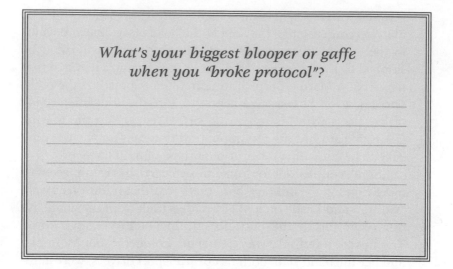

What's your biggest blooper or gaffe when you "broke protocol"?

767. Bloopers and gaffes when you "break protocol"

As a newlywed, my husband introduced me to people at a party our first week at our new duty station. When he said, "This is the Bos'n" (a Boatswain), I thought he said, "This is Mr. Bowson" (as in a last name). So I smiled, extended my hand, and said, "Nice to meet you, Mr. Bowson!" I'm sure I sounded like a four-year-old, but nobody told me I was an idiot.

–JOCELYN GREEN, author of *Faith Deployed: Daily Encouragement for Military Wives*

768. *Military Times* newspapers

Each week, the *Military Times* newsweeklies *Air Force Times, Army Times, Marine Corps Times,* and *Navy Times* are sold on military installations around the world.

>> **DID YOU KNOW?**

Military Times newspapers are the most purchased publications in AAFES and Defense Commissaries, beating such national bestsellers as *People* and *Time.*

769. *Stars and Stripes*

Stars and Stripes was first published during the American Civil War. The newspaper has been published continuously in Europe since 1942 and in the Pacific since 1945.

During World War I, *Stars and Stripes* was an eight-page weekly that reached a peak of 526,000 readers, relying on the improvisational efforts of its staff to get it printed in France and distributed to U.S. troops. Staff members were either veteran reporters or young soldiers who then often continued to work in publishing in the postwar years. For example, Harold Ross, editor of *Stars and Stripes*, returned home to found *The New Yorker* magazine.

During World War II, the newspaper was printed in dozens of editions in several operating theaters. Again, the staff included both newspapermen in uniform and soldiers who might later become important journalists. After Bill Mauldin did his popular *Willie and Joe* cartoons for the WWII *Stars and Stripes,* he went on to a successful career as an editorial cartoonist and twice won the Pulitzer Prize. Former *Stars and Stripes* staffers also include war correspondent Ernie Pyle and *60 Minutes'* Andy Rooney.

Today *Stars and Stripes* prints four editions daily, sold at military facilities overseas. The editions differ by theater, and include Europe, Japan, Korea, and the Middle East. The Mideast edition is distributed at no cost to Service members in contingency areas. In 2004, a digital edition was added. On any given day, the total average daily audience for *Stars and Stripes* is about 420,000.

See more at www.Stripes.com.

770. Military time—the 24-hour clock

771. Flags posted in front of the houses on military installations

772. Watches and bells

Mid Watch:	Midnight-0400
Morning Watch:	0400-0800
Forenoon Watch:	0800-1200
Afternoon Watch:	1200-1600
First Dog Watch:	1600-1800
Second Dog Watch:	1800-2000
Evening Watch:	2000-Midnight

Bells—Centuries-long tradition signaling the arrival or departure of important persons, keeping time, and sounding alarms

>>> **DID YOU KNOW?**

Naval tradition holds that the ship's cook shines the ship's bell and the ship's bugler shines the ship's whistle.

773. Staff rides—learning lessons from historic battles

Memorable moments, shared by Jack Scherer, U.S. Army Combat Engineer:

Gettysburg, Pickett's Charge: "Standing at the start point, thinking about the hot summer day, the wool uniforms, and the slope and distance those Confederate soldiers were asked to charge"

Normandy Beach: "Standing chest deep in the English Channel and charging the beach through the water without combat gear and not under fire, imagining how that day felt to the invaders"

774. "First Salute Coin"

When a newly commissioned officer receives his or her first salute, the officer gives that person a coin or a silver dollar.

Photo by Spc. Jonathan Montgomery

775. Military coins

An important part of preserving tradition

776. Operational Security (OPSEC) and Personal Security (PERSEC)

Careless Talk Costs Lives

Careless Talk ... Got There First

The *enemy* is listening. He wants to know what you know. Keep it to yourself.

Free Speech Doesn't Mean Careless Talk

Information Security Begins with You

Bits of Careless Talk Are Pieced Together by The Enemy

Loose Lips Might Sink Ships

Rumors Cost Us Lives

If you tell where they're going they may never get there.

He's Watching You

Someone Talked!

Normally, the enemy doesn't just ask for your critical information. Remember, OPSEC.

777. AFN commercials

I freely admit that I'm a total square. I actually prefer annoying AFN commercials to annoying real commercials that insinuate I'll be happier, hipper, sexier, and more successful if I buy this, use that, or shop there.

Call me crazy but I'd rather be badgered by people who aren't trying to sell me anything, except the ideas that I should exercise, eat right, stop smoking, eschew sexual harassment, wear a reflective belt, recycle, or call my chaplain if I'm gambling, drinking, stressed, or depressed.

When we return to life in CONUS, it's just possible that AFN ads will be among the things we'll recall when thinking of these good old days—even "Squeakers the Hamster" and "Chicken Knows Best."

Oh, the irony is not lost on me, I assure you.

–TERRI BARNES, Air Force spouse and *Spouse Calls* blog columnist

778. Halfway Night

Humor and wild antics!

What's your favorite Halfway Night memory?

Photo courtesy of 2nd Marine Logistics Group

Cpl. Sarah Webb of Combat Logistics Battalion 6, 2nd Marine Logistics Group, painted the first "Marine" rock at Fort Irwin and National Training Center, Calif.

779. Military mascots

780. The pride of standing and singing your Service's song
Especially in a room full of "brothers and sisters" from your branch
- Air Force: *Wild Blue Yonder*
- Army: *And the Army Goes Rolling Along*
- Coast Guard: *Semper Paratus (Always Ready)*
- Marine Corps: *From the Halls of Montezuma*
- Navy: *Anchors Aweigh*

781. Mustache March
Air Force Service members show solidarity by a symbolic, good-natured "protest" for one month against Air Force facial hair regulations. Some have contests held at the end of the month judging everyone's mustaches. Prizes are awarded for "Best Mustache," "Creepiest Mustache," "Honorary Membership in Law Enforcement," and "Most in Need of Testosterone Shot."

782. Military parades

Photo by Petty Officer 1st Class Mark O'Donald

Sailors from the USS *Samuel B. Roberts* march in the Bunker Hill Day parade in Boston.

You Know You're Part of the Military When ...

You are asked, "Excuse me, can you help me?
I'm looking for the In-Processing Center," and you
immediately think these directions make perfect sense:

"That's the PPC at the ACS building 3507. Turn left at
the PX, when you see building 4856 take a right, you'll
see ACS is across the street from the CDC building 3510.
If you've gone past the MP station you've gone too far."

783. Building numbers on military installations

784. Yellow ribbons— "Support Our Troops"

In the United States, yellow ribbons became popular during the
Iran hostage crisis. They were used as symbols of support for the
hostages. Yellow ribbons were featured prominently in the celebrations of their return home.

The modern-day yellow ribbons became popular during
the Gulf War in the early 1990s. It was during this time they appeared along with the slogan "Support Our Troops." Again in
2003 during the invasion of Iraq, yellow
ribbons appeared with similar meaning. You will find yellow ribbons to
show support of our troops tied
around trees, printed on magnetized
material affixed to automobiles, or
even in jewelry form as lapel pins.

★

Honor to the soldier and sailor everywhere,
who bravely bears his country's cause.
Honor, also, to the citizen who cares for
his brother in the field and serves,
as he best can, the same cause.

–ABRAHAM LINCOLN

★

OUTSIDE LOOKING IN

This nation will remain the land of the free,
only so long as it is the home of the brave.

–ELMER DAVIS, Director of the United States
Office of War Information during WWII

785. Inherited values

My father was military and still lives daily with the same
pride, patriotism, and practices of his time serving—
decades later. I inherited those strong morals and
characteristics from him, and I love him for it.

–SHERYL ROUSH, former Navy wife, coauthor of *Heart of a Military Woman*

786. Experiencing the incredible "quiet professionalism" and politeness of our Service members—"Let me help you, ma'am."

Patriotism is not short, frenzied outbursts of emotion,
but the tranquil and steady dedication of a lifetime.

–ADLAI E. STEVENSON

787. Feeling grateful when you see someone in the military
Knowing they are heroes worthy of admiration and respect

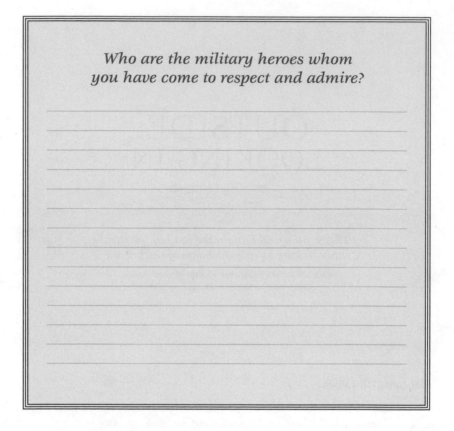

*Who are the military heroes whom
you have come to respect and admire?*

788. Federal Voting Assistance Program

Voting help for uniformed Service members, their families, and other citizens living outside the United States

See more at www.fvap.gov.

789. The difference military members and their families make to so many civilian charities and programs through the Combined Federal Campaign

790. Toys for Tots

Former Marines step up to provide a sign of hope to economically disadvantaged children at Christmas.

791. Getting to hear all the good things our military is doing in places like Iraq and Afghanistan

As I begin my final week here in Afghanistan, I pause to consider the selfless dedication of all our men and women serving so far from home.

As I have moved around the country, I have witnessed an amazing work ethic and positive attitudes, even in the face of fierce combat, difficult living conditions, long hours, little sleep, and very few creature comforts.

As for the broader aspects of this war, one might easily be discouraged if they listen to those who are opining without being here to see all the positive changes that have occurred. Even in my short five months, I've seen significant progress and increased levels of security. Those who were here just two short years ago can't believe the freedom the Afghans now have and how they are improving their situation.

I've heard Afghan police, military, and political leaders alike talk about their desire to end corruption, their confidence about defeating the insurgents, and their yearning to get their country back on its feet and reduce outside support. I also routinely hear reports of the increasingly successful and courageous acts of the Afghan national police and army forces.

To be sure, there is a lot yet to accomplish and some very serious fighting ahead. There is, however, even more to be confident of, not the least of which is the indomitable spirit of our Soldiers, Sailors, Airmen, and Marines, and those who support them.

Although I am anxious to return home, it is difficult to leave in the middle of something so historic and in which one can palpably sense the positive change, and know that this year will tell the difference. Mostly, I hate to leave the incredibly devoted team I have worked with, the dedicated civilians willing to take risk, and those magnificent men and women in uniform that protect us. I've been blessed to be a part of this.

–MAJ. GEN. DON RILEY, U.S. Army, April 25, 2010

792. Embedded journalists—press ride-alongs

You know one of the really amazing things about the guys out there is that they also understood that they were fighting for people who opposed the war, and they accepted that. Their tolerance is something society at home would do well to emulate.

The group bond was incredibly strong. As one soldier said, "There are guys in the platoon that outright hate each other, but they would all die for each other." So he's talking about a brotherhood, rather than a friendship, that is particularly profound and which adds a lot of significance and meaning to their lives. It's no wonder they come home and actually miss being "out there," a fact that most civilians can't get their heads around.

–TIM HETHERINGTON, a photographer embedded with the soldiers at Outpost Restrepo in the Korengal Valley of Afghanistan in 2007, was killed April 20, 2011, while covering the conflict in Misrata, Libya.

793. Medal of Honor recipients—the nation's highest military award

Don't call Staff Sgt. Salvatore "Sal" Giunta a hero. Don't say that he went above and beyond the call of duty when he single-handedly stopped two terrorists from kidnapping his wounded buddy during a ferocious firefight in Afghanistan in 2007. Don't try to tell him his actions were in any way extraordinary or that he's anything but an average Soldier. Because, as Giunta sees it, he was just doing his job. He didn't do anything that any other paratrooper in 1st Platoon, Battle Company, 173rd Airborne Brigade Combat Team—or anyone in the U.S. military for that matter—wouldn't have done, and he can't quite understand the fuss.

"I didn't do anything other than what I was supposed to. I know two men personally gave every single tomorrow they'll ever have. This is for everyone who has been to Iraq, everyone who has been to Afghanistan, everyone who has to suck it up for a while without their family, and it's about the families who have to suck it up when their husband or wife is deployed. This is for all of us. This is for everyone who sacrifices for their country, who sacrifices for America."

–ELIZABETH M. COLLINS, "Reluctant hero: Soldier becomes first living MOH recipient since Vietnam." *Soldiers* magazine, March 1, 2011

★ ★

Special Days to Honor the Military

794. Freedom Day—February 1

Fitting, isn't it, that the year starts out with a celebration of freedom? Typically, we identify the Fourth of July as America's Independence or Freedom Day. But this *other* Freedom Day has different origins. According to CultureofPeace.org, this is an opportunity not just to celebrate freedom but to "rededicate our commitment to work for *freedom* for all." President Harry Truman proclaimed February 1 as National Freedom Day in 1948. The date was chosen because it was the day that President Abraham Lincoln signed the Thirteenth Amendment, abolishing and prohibiting slavery. Former slaves and their descendants had celebrated this day unofficially since 1865.

Our Service members are often referred to as Freedom Fighters, for our nation and for other nations as well.

795. Patriot's Day in April—a day to remember the Revolutionary War

796. April—Month of the Military Child

When Service members are deployed, they leave many loved ones behind, including children, who lose precious time with their parents and whose home lives are disrupted by the frequent moves and deployments associated with military life. Thus, it's been said that when parents serve, children serve too. This month is for them.

Connect and Join Inc. has brought to light an effort to make this month fun for military children and a learning experience for corporate and educational institution partners. Their website, www.monthofthemilitarychild.com, offers event suggestions and project and lesson plans for educators. Parents can join in the celebration by visiting the site for arts and crafts projects with a military flair.

797. Loyalty Day and Silver Star Day—May 1

Loyalty Day is a day to reflect on that specific virtue and to rededicate ourselves as loyal Americans. America wouldn't be the same without loyal citizens.

Silver Star Day is observed by the Silver Star Families of America (SSFOA), a loyal volunteer organization that serves our injured and ill Service members. It's not that they serve only Silver Star recipients, but rather that silver is the color that denotes all injured/ill Service members, just as blue stars denote all Service members and gold denotes those killed in action.

798. May—National Military Appreciation Month

799. Military Spouse Appreciation Day—Friday before Mother's Day in May

This day of honor for all military spouses was first proclaimed by President Ronald Reagan in 1984. It's grown rapidly in recent years, in light of the relentless pressures on military spouses because of the war on terrorism. Some organizations and businesses host dinners for military spouses, feature discounts or sales, or perform services to make this day more meaningful.

800. Armed Forces Day in May

Armed Forces Day is the culmination of Armed Forces Week, which starts the second Saturday in May. This day is set aside for all services to combine their celebrations of continued existence and service.

801. Memorial Day—last Monday in May

>> **DID YOU KNOW?**

Just prior to Memorial Day weekend, every available soldier in the 3rd U.S. Infantry (The Old Guard) places small American flags at each of the more than 260,000 gravestones at Arlington National Cemetery. They then patrol twenty-four hours a day during the weekend to ensure that each flag remains standing.

In a tradition conducted since 1948, a member of the 3rd U.S. Infantry Regiment places flags at gravestones at Arlington National Cemetery, Va., for Memorial Day.

802. Flag Day—June 14

Flying the flag is highly encouraged from this day through the Fourth of July.

803. Independence Day—July 4

804. POW/MIA Recognition Day—third Friday in September

The National League of Families worked to gain this day of recognition to remember our prisoners of war and those missing in action. Each year the president orders a proclamation and requires federal buildings to fly the POW/MIA flag professing the claim, "You are not forgotten."

805. Gold Star Mother's Day—last Sunday in September

Gold Star Mothers are those who lost a son or daughter in service to our country. This organization is eighty years old and was established shortly after WWI.

806. November—Military Family Month

807. Veterans Day—November 11

Do you know the difference between Memorial Day and Veterans Day?

Many people confuse Memorial Day and Veterans Day. Memorial Day is a day for remembering and honoring military personnel who died in service to their country. Veterans Day is set aside to thank and honor all those who served honorably in the military—in wartime or peacetime. Veterans Day is largely intended to thank living veterans for their military service, and to underscore the fact that everyone who served—not only those who died—have sacrificed and done their duty.

808. Gold Star Wives Day—established in 2010 as December 18

★ ★

809. Corporations that see the value in hiring and keeping military spouses as part of their workforce, offering real careers

TOP TEN MILITARY-SPOUSE FRIENDLY EMPLOYERS—2011
Courtesy of *Military Spouse* magazine

- United Services Automobile Association (USAA)
- TriWest Healthcare Alliance
- T-Mobile
- Army and Air Force Exchange (AAFES)
- CSC
- Adecco
- RE/MAX, LLC
- The Home Depot
- Health Net Inc.
- Kelly Services

810. Benefiting from the works of the Corps of Engineers

U.S. Army Corps of Engineer (USACE) military officers, together with their civilian force, protect U.S. lakes and waterways and provide public recreational areas throughout the country. They also work with the Federal Emergency Management Agency in responding to national disasters such as Hurricane Katrina, flooding along the Mississippi River, or tornadoes. Similarly, the Naval Civil Engineer Corps (CEC) maintains our shoreline facilities. The Corps of Engineers also takes on the challenges of managing construction around the world in support of American foreign policy, building everything from roads to schools and power plants in countries like Iraq and Afghanistan, and other places in Europe and Asia.

> *One of the impressive things to me about the U.S. Army Corps of Engineers is the commitment and passion for mission shown by the civilians! Many (and their families) are very willing to take the sacrifice and risk, and some, heroically and sadly, have made the ultimate sacrifice. The Army and the nation benefit daily from their extraordinary efforts.*

> –ROZ RILEY, Army wife of former Deputy Chief of Engineers and Deputy Commanding General of USACE

811. The many military members who volunteer their time after duty hours— yes, even in war zones

Service members have done everything from collecting such basic essentials as blankets, school supplies, and jackets to teaching adults and children. Others coach soccer and raise awareness of local or national needs and garner support from those back home. Service members have volunteered their off-duty time in Iraq and Afghanistan and in many other countries during peacetime deployments as well.

To give just one example:
While deployed with the U.S. Marine Corps to Romania and Bulgaria, Staff Sgt. Aaron Weiss saw an opportunity to make a difference for an orphanage in Constanta, Romania. Noting the run-down and actually dangerous playground, he coordinated with the U.S. Embassy to take on a volunteer project to renovate the playground.

As he reported in an article in the National Military Family Association's newsletter, "I asked for volunteers from the USMC unit to donate their few weekend off-days to take on this project, and I was surprised to have such an overwhelming response to this call for help. We had no shortage of helping hands."

812. The many inventions and developments because of the military that have benefited society as a whole

- The Internet
- Advances in prosthetics
- Jet engines
- Thermal imaging devices
- Radars
- Submarines
- Extensive research on treatment of post-traumatic stress disorder

Photo by Steve Vanderwerff

813. Wreaths Across America

The Arlington Wreath program was started in 1992 by Morrill Worcester with the donation and laying of 5,000 Christmas wreaths in Arlington National Cemetery. It has become an annual journey for Mr. Worcester. In 2005, thousands of requests poured in from all over the country from people wanting to emulate the Arlington project at their national and state cemeteries, spurring the creation of "Wreaths Across America."

By 2008, more than three hundred locations held wreath-laying ceremonies in every state, Puerto Rico, and twenty-four overseas cemeteries. More than 100,000 wreaths were placed on veterans' graves, and more than 60,000 volunteers participated.

Remember—the fallen; Honor—those who serve; Teach—children the value of freedom.

> *Freedom is never more than one generation away from extinction. We didn't pass it to our children in the bloodstream. It must be fought for, protected, and handed on for them to do the same, or one day we will spend our sunset years telling our children and our children's children what it was once like in the United States where men were free.*

–RONALD REAGAN

814. Interservice rivalries

815. Service school rivalries

>>> **DID YOU KNOW?**

Navy Midshipman (and later Admiral) Joseph Mason Reeves wore the first football helmet in 1893 during the Army-Navy Game. He was told by a Navy doctor that if he were kicked in the head one more time, he could be risking his life or "instant insanity." Reeves commissioned an Annapolis shoemaker to make him a helmet out of leather.

816. Military Academy football games

SOME HIGHLIGHTS

- Watching the cadets and midshipmen do push-ups during their games after a touchdown
- Commander-in-Chief trophy
- Realizing that few, if any, of the cadets or midshipmen will ever play in the NFL. They're playing because they love the game.
- Admiring the sense of respect and solidarity the Academy teams have for one another—by watching all the players at the end of the game singing each other's alma mater. Where else would you see this type of sportsmanship?
- Feeling pride when you hear others recognize what it means to be a student-athlete. During a televised game between the Navy and San Diego on Dec. 23, 2010, one of the announcers said in awe: "These Navy players are true student-athletes; their GPAs are off the charts."

817. Recruiters

818. Recruiting partnerships with NASCAR

There's an awesome thrill watching those *cars in uniform* speed around the track. Off the track, cars like No. 43 (Air Force) and No. 88 (National Guard) make the rounds to participate in recruiting efforts like school visits and swear-ins of new recruits.

Photo Courtesy U.S. Army Europe

819. Presidential directive, "Strengthening Our Military Families," January 24, 2011, outlining how federal agencies are supporting military families

So we are here today because nearly a decade of war has been taking place, and our Armed Forces—you and your families—have done everything you've been asked to do. You've been everything we could ask you to be. You have done your duty. And as a grateful nation, we must do ours. We have to make sure that America is serving you as well as you have served us ...

We also recognize that this can't be a mission for government alone. Government has its responsibilities, but one percent of Americans may be fighting our wars; one hundred percent of Americans need to be supporting our troops and their families—one hundred percent ...

I want every single American to remember that as the beneficiaries of their service, each of us has an obligation—a sacred duty—to care for those who have "borne the battle."

–BARACK OBAMA

820. Wearing red poppies and little blue forget-me-nots to honor those who have been injured or have made the ultimate sacrifice for our country

The idea of wearing red poppies and forget-me-nots came from the poem "In Flanders Fields," written in 1915 by John McCrae, and from the memories of soldiers from World War I who had seen spring flowers growing on the graves of comrades and allies killed in the fighting. These two flowers soon became the accepted symbol for commemorating our veterans.

The red poppies have traditionally been worn on Memorial Day to honor those who gave their lives for our country. Many felt the best way to honor the dead was to assist those who came home bearing the scars of war, and in 1926, the nonprofit organization Disabled American Veterans started using the little blue forget-me-not as a fund-raising symbol to support disabled veterans.

821. The unifying attitude of "Support Our Troops!"

This sentiment seems to be the one thing that just about everyone can agree on—supporting our Service men and women.

I think my admiration comes for both the families that support and stand by their loved ones through the highs and lows of living a military life. But my admiration and gratitude extends to the Servicemen and women that are risking their lives every day to stand true to their love for their country and the futures of generations to come. I don't think that you have to particularly be part of a military to have pride in our [Service members] and the people that support them.

–VANESSA, AWN Facebook fan

822. JoiningForces.gov—First Lady Michelle Obama and Dr. Jill Biden's initiative to reach out to military families

Everyone can do something.

We're not going to stop until every part of our society —every part, both inside and outside of government— is fully mobilized to support our troops and their families.

–MICHELLE OBAMA

What are some ways you can "join forces"?

Photo by Seaman Apprentice John Scorza

Service members spread the American flag across Qualcomm Stadium at halftime during the San Diego Chargers' twentieth annual Military Appreciation night.

823. Military Appreciation Days at sports games, auto races, concert halls

824. Military-inspired fashion for the whole family

Berets, epaulets, dog tags, aviators, cargo pants, and pea coats, to name a few. Now there are even flight suits and dog tags for kids.

825. Flagpoles

First used to assist military coordination and identification on the battlefield or at sea

826. Service school alumni

Ensuring that the legacy of the school lives on through networking, raising awareness, and providing funds for facilities and scholarships

827. Motivational and inspirational military speeches

★ ★

Special Ways Civilians Support Our Troops

828. Adopt a Soldier, Adopt a Platoon, and care-package givers extraordinaire

829. Wire a Cake

Each month Wire a Cake adopts a Service member (through the Soldiers' Angels organization) and sends him or her a cake, cookies, or pie. You can order and customize your own, anytime.

See more at www.wireacake.com/militarycakes.html.

830. Cell Phones for Soldiers

See more at www.cellphonesforsoldiers.com.

831. Free signs from Build A Sign

See more at www.buildasign.com/troops.

832. Free doulas—for pregnant military spouses of deployed Service members

See more at www.operationspecialdelivery.com.

833. Soldiers' Angels

Started by Patti Patton-Bader, a self-described ordinary mother of two American soldiers. In 2003 when her son expressed concern that some soldiers in his unit did not receive any mail or support from home, Patti went into action and began the mission of Soldiers' Angels, "May No Soldier Go Unloved." In addition to sending care packages, their mission expanded to wounded warriors to include programs like these:
- Heroes and Horses
- Voice-controlled/adaptive laptops to wounded Service members
- Blankets of Hope sewing teams

Photo by Allison Chastain

834. *Sesame Street Talk, Listen, Connect* DVD—to help children who are dealing with deployments

835. Our Military Kids—a program to help the children of the National Guard and Reserve

Comfort. Stability. Routine. Fun! All children need these ingredients to thrive but especially those who have a parent deployed in military service to our country or recovering from injury at home.

Along with the sacrifice of having a parent away in service for months at a time, many Guard and Reserve families are so financially stretched they cannot afford the fees for sports, fine arts, or tutoring programs so crucial to their children's sense of well-being. Children of wounded warriors face similar financial difficulties along with the challenges of learning to adapt to the physical, mental, and emotional changes in a loved one.

Our Military Kids, founded in 2004, stepped in to meet these needs with a simple grant program that pays for children's activities. Our Military Kids has distributed grants to children in all fifty states, the District of Columbia, and all U.S. territories. See more at www.ourmilitarykids.org.

★ ★

More Ways Civilians Serve Those Who Serve

836. Fisher Houses—"a home away from home" for families of patients receiving medical care at major military and VA medical centers

Imagine what it would be like to have your military member, spouse, or child in a hospital far away from home. What if you didn't have friends or family nearby to stay with and couldn't afford a hotel? Fisher House steps in to help.

In 1990, Pauline Trost, wife of Chief of Naval Operations Admiral Carlisle Trost, presented the need for temporary lodging facilities for families at major military centers to philanthropists Zachary and Elizabeth Fisher. One year later, President George Bush dedicated the first Fisher House at the National Naval Medical Center, Bethesda, Maryland.

A month later, a house at Forest Glen Annex to Walter Reed Army Medical Center opened, followed by one at Wilford Medical Center in San Antonio, Texas. Based on the success of these houses, the Fishers decided to expand the program beyond the initial gift of one house for each military service. By the time of Zachary Fisher's death in 1999, he and Elizabeth had personally financed more than twenty Fisher Houses.

They established the Fisher House Foundation Inc. in 1993 as a national not-for-profit organization designed to assist in the coordination of private support and public support for the Fisher House program.

In 2001, the Fisher House Foundation joined forces with the Defense Commissary Agency to provide financial grants through their Scholarships for Military Children program. In 2004, they partnered with "Operation Hero Miles," expanding the program to include free air travel to enable hospitalized Service members to go on leave or pass from military medical centers, and to allow their families and friends to visit at the medical centers.

In 2010, twenty years after Pauline Trost's initial request, the Fisher Foundation has served more than 142,000 families and provided more than 3.6 million days of lodging, saving families more than $167 million in lodging and transportation costs. There are now fifty-three Fisher Houses located in eighteen military installations and fifteen VA medical centers. Twelve more houses are under construction or in design, and a list of future homes that are needed has been developed.

837. The Sierra Club alliance

A program "to ensure that those military families making the greatest sacrifice for our country are given the opportunity to benefit from the healing powers of our natural heritage"

- **Military Families Outdoors program**: In partnership with the National Military Family Association and the Armed Services YMCA, offers a free week of summer fun for military kids with parents who have been, are currently, or will be deployed

- **Outward Bound**: Experiences allow soldiers to connect with nature, challenge themselves, and spend time with other veterans away from the battlefield, at no cost.

838. Sears' "Heroes at Home" program

Provides support to military Service members, veterans, and their families through joint efforts with various nonprofit organizations and through the "Heroes at Home" Wish Registry

839. Armed Services YMCA

Provides an array of programs and discounts for military Service members and their families. ASYMCA even provides free respite child care at participating YMCA locations for families of deployed Service members.

See more at www.asymca.org.

840. Operation Homefront

Provides direct services to alleviate a military family's or individual's actual/complete emergency financial burden, as well as counseling and/or recovery support. Where there is a need they cannot provide, they will partner with others for the benefit of military families.

One easy way for families and communities to support our troops and the families they leave behind is through a division of Operation Homefront called eCarePackage. Baby items, books and crosswords, clothing, gift cards, and more can be bought from the eCarePackage store (www.eCarePackage.org) and donated to adopted families on the home front.

See more at www.operationhomefront.org.

841. Thanks USA

Provides college, technical, and vocational scholarships for children and spouses of Service members. The idea for this organization came from two young sisters wanting to find a way to thank the troops. Their program uses a treasure hunt based on American history and values to help raise awareness for scholarships.

See more at www.thanksusa.org.

842. Armed Forces Foundation (AFF)

A nonprofit organization providing financial support, career counseling, housing assistance, and recreational therapy programs. For example, AFF has donated about $10,000 a month to the Navy Lodge at the National Naval Medical Center to offset expenses for families visiting loved ones.

See more at www.armedforcesfoundation.org.

843. Interstate Compact on Education Opportunity for Children

A growing initiative aimed at easing the transition of military children to new schools when they move from state to state

844. Free nights of rest and relaxation

- **Salute to Soldiers**

  www.salutetosoldiers.com

  The Asian American Hotel Owners Association (AAHOA) recognizes that freedom is not free. To honor the service and sacrifice of our troops, AAHOA works with the USO to provide Service members and their families with free nights of rest and relaxation through its "Salute to Soldiers" program.

- **Operation R&R**

  www.operationrestandrelax.org

  A nonprofit organization designed to give Service members an opportunity to reconnect with their spouses and children upon their return from Iraq or Afghanistan. Property owners, represented by many property management companies, donate their homes and villas on Hilton Head Island, South Carolina, for this purpose. This is all to ensure that our military families have a chance to spend some time away from their everyday lives to strengthen relationships that have been strained during long separations and under extreme circumstances.

★ ★

★ ★

"Never leave a fallen comrade behind."

Duty, Honor, Country.
We must never forget those thousands of Americans
who, with their courage, with their sacrifice,
and with their lives, made those words live
for all of us.

–SEN. JOHN MCCAIN

Photo by Sgt. 1st Class Mark Burrell

Army Spc. Brit B. Jacobs, with the 101st Airborne Division, gives a farewell kiss to the helmet of a fallen comrade during a memorial service in Kunar province, Afghanistan.

845. Wounded Warriors Foundation

846. Intrepid Fallen Heroes Fund

Raises funds for important centers for wounded warriors medical services

See more at www.fallenheroesfund.org.

847. Readjustment support

See more at www.vettrauma.org.

848. The Coming Home Project

See more at www.cominghomeproject.org.

849. One Freedom

This remarkable team of field experts provides a powerful framework of education and training that builds strength, resilience, and a clearer understanding of how to maintain balance in the face of military deployments and other lifestyle challenges.

See more at www.onefreedom.org.

850. Bob Woodruff Foundation

As an anchor for ABC News, Bob Woodruff suffered a traumatic brain injury (TBI) caused by a roadside bomb in 2006 while he was traveling with an Army unit in Iraq. Following his long recovery, the Woodruffs started the Bob Woodruff Foundation in 2008 to raise awareness of hidden injuries like TBI, PTSD, and combat-stress-related issues. Bob's wife, Lee, coauthor with him of *In an Instant,* a book about that time, said they wanted to find something positive in their experience to show their children that good things can come from bad. The foundation aims to get Americans involved, engaged, and aware of the price paid by military families.

See more at at www.remind.org.

851. Sew Much Comfort

Provides free adaptive clothing to support the needs of injured Service members

See more at www.sewmuchcomfort.org.

>>> **DID YOU KNOW?**

Did you know these interesting Military.com facts?

10,000,000	Military.com has 10 million members.
20,000,000	Search more than 20 million records for military buddies with Buddy Finder.
35,000	Search more than 35,000 unit pages, find reunions, and correspond with old friends.
4,000	Search the database of 4,000 institutions and find your school now with School Finder.
1,000	Search more than 1,000 scholarships and find millions of dollars with Scholarship Finder.

852. Military.com

The online presence of Military Advantage is committed to the mission of connecting the military community to all the advantages earned in service to America. Military Advantage is a division of Monster Worldwide.

853. Hope for the Warriors

See more at www.hopeforthewarriors.org.

854. Achilles' Freedom Team of Wounded Veterans

This program brings running programs and marathon opportunities to disabled veterans returning from Iraq and Afghanistan.

See more at www.achillesinternational.org/programs/freedom-team/overview.

855. Circles of Change

In this unique program, wounded warriors work with rescued dogs.

See more at www.circle-of-change.org/VP/index.htm.

856. Homes for Our Troops

A national nonprofit organization founded in 2004 to provide homes for severely injured Service members and their immediate families by raising donations to cover the costs of building materials and professional labor. The homes provided by Homes for Our Troops are given to the veterans at no cost.

857. Service dogs and therapy dogs—some of the most popular therapists for wounded warriors

- Tower of Hope www.thetowerofhope.org
- Canines for Combat Veterans www.neads.org
- Canine Companions for Independence www.cci.org
- Hawaii Fi-Do www.hawaiifido.org
- Red Cross Pet Therapy Program

> My dog Tootsie is a certified pet therapy dog. For the past two and a half years, we have provided pet therapy at Walter Reed Army Medical Center, the Malogne House, DeWitt Army Hospital, and Portsmouth Naval Medical Center. Visiting wounded Service members and their families has a special place in my heart. I understand what they are going through, having gone through it with our son. Many of the patients miss their pets at home, so seeing Tootsie brings a piece of home to their day. Tootsie brings smiles and comfort everywhere she goes, helping patients forget about their pain and worries for a little while. It might sound strange, but I can tell Tootsie knows it's an honor to visit these brave Service members and their families and has a great respect and admiration for them. Visiting wounded Service members and their families and other patients throughout the hospital with Tootsie is a small way I can give back for their sacrifices. It's another way to serve my country. I feel blessed to have met so many wonderful and courageous people during our visits.
>
> –LINDA ODIERNO, Army wife and Army volunteer, advisor and mentor

858. The National Intrepid Center of Excellence

Located in Bethesda, Maryland, the center was built entirely with private donations. This state-of-the-art research, diagnosis, and treatment center, offers care for wounded heroes suffering from traumatic brain injury and psychological health conditions.

859. Voices for America's Troops Program

The group's purpose is to support a strong national defense and sustain a top-quality all-volunteer force by ensuring fair treatment of all who serve in uniform—past, present, and future—and their families and survivors. The primary purpose of Voices is to educate the public on legislative and policy challenges affecting the military and veterans community.

America's troops and their dedicated families are the only military weapon system that has never let our country down. Voices is dedicated to ensuring America continues to provide them with the same level of reciprocal support and commitment that they have consistently demonstrated for America.

See more at www.voicesfortroops.org.

860. American Red Cross

Since the days of Clara Barton, the American Red Cross has been a friend to the military. They link military families during a crisis and care for our wounded. Moreover, they constantly create new ways to support and serve the military population with such new programs as Psychological First Aid training and Safe and Well online communications.

See more at www.redcross.org.

★ ★

★ ★

"Never forget the sacrifice."

Let us not mourn that such men died,
but rejoice that such men lived.

–GEN. GEORGE S. PATTON JR.

861. Tragedy Assistance Program for Survivors (TAPS)

Founded in 1994, TAPS has established itself as the 24/7 front line resource for anyone who has suffered the loss of a military loved one. Their National Military Survivor Seminars and Good Grief camps are held across the country, providing ongoing emotional help, hope, and healing to all who are grieving the death of a Service member.

See more at www.taps.org.

862. Honor and Remember

See more at www.honorandremember.org.

863. Gold Star Families

One percent of Americans are touched by this war.
Then there is a much smaller club of families
who have given all.

–LT. GEN. JOHN KELLY, U.S. Marine Corps, father of 2nd Lt. Robert M. Kelly, 29, who was killed in Afghanistan

864. Fallen Heroes Project by Michael Reagan

This artist is making portraits of our fallen heroes for their family members—for free.

865. Project Compassion

Kaziah and other portrait artists at HeroPaintings.com make sure our fallen soldiers are "seen" and never forgotten.

★ ★

866. Famous Military Art

Artists' renderings of military life are something to ponder and admire. Some artists have become favorites in our homes and are even commissioned by the military to be put on permanent display at bases the world over.

SOME EXAMPLES

- WWII nose art on airplanes
- Jasper Johns' flags
- Dru Blair's aviation paintings
- Dale Gallon's Civil War prints and historical art
- Todd Krasovetz's art commissions
- T. Branson's "Hands," Pentagon series

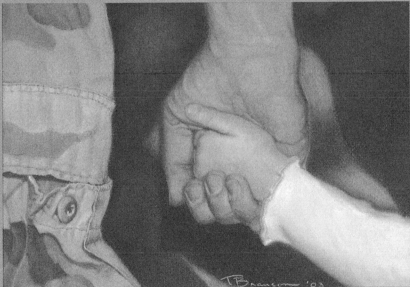

Photo and original artwork by T Branson

Green Ramp (2003) is the first of several military paintings by T Branson. Inspired by a photo of her Special Forces nephew holding his daughter's hand before a deployment, it represents every parent wearing the uniform of America's Armed Forces who has ever had to hold his or her child's hand and say "good-bye."

867. Military-inspired comic strips, comic books

THEIR CREATORS

- *Up Front* by Bill Mauldin
  He was one of the foremost cartoonists of the twentieth century. As an Infantryman in the U.S. Army 45th Division, he brought his experiences to life in his *Up Front* comic strip with Joe and Willie. He volunteered to draw cartoons for the unit's newspaper, and it wasn't long until his work was picked up by *Stars and Stripes*. His single-panel strips were published from 1940 until 1991—when he stopped drawing. The comic earned him his first Pulitzer prize in 1945 (making him the youngest person to win a Pulitzer prize). His second Pulitzer Prize was awarded in 1959.

- *Beetle Bailey* by Mort Walker (1951-present)

- *Sad Sack* by George Baker

- *GI Joe* by Dave Breger
  Before Hasbro created the GI Joe action figures in 1964, Dave Breger introduced GI Joe in his comic strips in 1942.

>>> DID YOU KNOW?

In the 1940s, American GIs were the second largest audience for comic books after young readers.

- *Sgt. Rock* by Robert Kanigher (1959-1988)
- Dr. Seuss
  In his role as an Army illustrator during WWII, Dr. Seuss produced *This Is Ann*, an educational comic book for soldiers. Ann is an *Anopheles* mosquito whose bite brings on a bad case of malaria. He also created a character, the Squander Bug, "an evil pest that gobbles money that should be spent for War Bonds and War Stamps."

MORE RECENT COMICS

- *Air Force Blues* by Staff Sgt. Austin M. May
- *Broadside* by Jeff Bacon
- *Gunston Street Comics* by Basil Zaviski
- *INCOMING!* by John Sheppard
- *Jenny the Military Spouse and Friends* by Julie Negron, the only female and military spouse cartoonist on the list
- *PVT Murphy's Law* by Mark V. Baker
- *SemperToons* by GySgt Wolf
- *Ricky's Tour* by Mike Jones
- *Pope's Pun* by W. C. Pope
- *Downrange* by Jeffery Hall
- *GeeDunk* by Jeff Hobrath
- *FNG* by Gary Sullivan
- *Combatoons* by Luke Marble
- *Ft. Knox* by Paul Jon

868. Military-inspired video games

- *America's Army*
- *Call of Duty*
- *Medal of Honor*
- *Battlefield*

869. Military-inspired movies

AIR FORCE MOVIES
- *Wings* (1927)
- *Air Force* (1943)
- *Twelve O'clock High* (1949)
  also a TV series (1960s)
- *No Time for Sergeants* (1958)
  also a book, Broadway play,
  and TV sitcom
- *A Gathering of Eagles* (1963)
- *Dr. Strangelove* (1964)
- *The Right Stuff* (1983)
- *The Tuskegee Airmen* (1995)

ARMY MOVIES
- *All Quiet on the Western Front* (1930)
- *Sergeant York* (1941)
- *White Christmas* (1954)
- *Hell and Back* (1955)
- *The Bridge on the River Kwai* (1957)
- *The Longest Day* (1962)
- *The Dirty Dozen* (1967)
- *The Green Berets* (1968)
- *Patton* (1970)
- *MASH* (1970)
- *Apocalypse Now* (1979)
- *Private Benjamin* (1980)
- *Platoon* (1986)
- *Glory* (1989)
- *Renaissance Man* (1994)
- *Saving Private Ryan* (1998)
- *Black Hawk Down* (2001)
- *We Were Soldiers* (2002)
- *The Hurt Locker* (2008)
- *Restrepo* (2010)

COAST GUARD MOVIES
- *Sea Devils* (1937)
- *Coast Guard* (1939)
- *Tars and Spars* (1946)
- *Fighting Coast Guard* (1951)
- *Sea of Lost Ships* (1953)
- *The Perfect Storm* (2000)
- *The Guardian* (2006)

MARINE CORPS MOVIES
- *Tell It to the Marines* (1926)
- *Gung Ho!* (1943)
- *Pride of the Marines* (1945)
- *Sands of Iwo Jima* (1949)
- *Coming Home* (1978)
- *Heartbreak Ridge* (1986)
- *Full Metal Jacket* (1987)
- *Born on the Fourth of July* (1989)
- *A Few Good Men* (1992)
- *Flags of Our Fathers* (2006)
- *Letters from Iwo Jima* (2006)

NAVY MOVIES
- *The Fighting Seabees* (1944)
- *They Were Expendable* (1945)
- *Mister Roberts* (1955)
- *The Caine Mutiny* (1954)
- *Father Goose* (1964)
- *Tora! Tora! Tora!* (1970)
- *Midway* (1976)
- *An Officer and A Gentleman* (1982)
- *Top Gun* (1986)
- *The Hunt for Red October* (1990)
- *Crimson Tide* (1995)

870. Military-inspired television shows

Without which some civilians may never "see inside"

COMEDY
- Sgt. Bilko (1955-1959)
  also a movie (1996)
- McHale's Navy (1962-1966)
  also a movie (1964 and 1997)
- Gomer Pyle (1964-1969)
- Hogan's Heroes (1965-1971)
- MASH (1972-1983)
- Roll Out (1973)
- C.P.O. Sharkey (1976-1978)
- Operation Petticoat (1977-1978)
- Major Dad (1989-1993)

DRAMA
- Combat (1962-1967)
- Twelve O'clock High (1964-1967)

- The Rat Patrol (1966-1968)
- Tour of Duty (1987-1990)
- China Beach (1988-1991)
- JAG (1995-2005)
- NCIS (2003-present)
- The Unit (2006-2009)
- Army Wives (2007-present)

TV MINISERIES
- Generation Kill (2008)
- Over There (2005)
- Band of Brothers (2001)
- Taking Chance (2009)
- The Pacific (2010)

What are your favorite military-inspired movies and television shows?

871. Heart-centered songs by artists who may not be household names but share their life experiences through music

These songs help others have a better understanding of what life in the military is all about.

- "Keep Living" by Heather Wagner, Air Force spouse. "Until the day he makes it home I'll take care of things on my own. When he's here he'll be glad to see that we just kept living."

- "American by God's Amazing Grace" by Luke Stricklin, former Army soldier. He struggled trying to explain his experiences in Iraq to his family and friends back home who asked him what it was like to fight in Baghdad. He couldn't speak the words very well, but he could sing them. His song hit the country music charts and a new career began.

- "Flags Of Our Fathers" by Keni Thomas, country singer and former U.S. Army Ranger who served in the Battle of Mogadishu. He donates portions of the sales of his album to the Hero Fund, which helps Special Operation Warriors. Keni Thomas is also a national speaker sharing his motivating message of teamwork and leadership.

- "So Brave" written by Angela Lashley, a mother of a soldier, for her son. It was featured in *Army Times* newspapers as "A Soldier's Mother's Anthem."

> *When I walked out of church the Sunday following the tragedy [Sept. 11], people were humming "America the Beautiful" and asking each other if they could remember all the verses of "The Star-Spangled Banner." We turn and return to the words we share, words that have inspired Americans in the past, and that have been passed down to us. Knowing that they aided our parents and grandparents in overcoming the horrors of war helps give us the confidence that we need to fight our generation's battle for freedom and democracy.*
>
> –CAROLINE KENNEDY, *A Patriot's Handbook*

What are your favorite songs?

872. The comforting feeling of being in a civilian world and seeing a Service member in uniform

873. Key military campaigns

On December 22, 1944, during the Battle of the Bulge in World War II, Anthony Clement McAuliffe was acting commander of the 101st Airborne Division in charge of the defense of Bastogne, Belgium. The Americans were surrounded. The advancing German forces called on McAuliffe's garrison to surrender. Instead, McAuliffe sent back a note: "To the German Commander: NUTS! The American Commander." Bastogne was successfully held by the Americans.

Photo by Gary Nichols/Released

National Naval Aviation Museum

874. Museums

- National Naval Aviation Museum
- Marine Corps Air-Ground Museum
- D-Day Museum
- U.S. Army Women's Museum
- U.S. Air Force Museum
- National Civil War Museum
- USS *Constitution* Museum
- USCGC Eagle Museum
- Airborne and Special Operations Museum
- American Helicopter Museum
- Frontier Army Museum
- Strategic Air Command Museum
- U.S. Army Medical Department Museum
- Naval Undersea Museum
- White Sands Missile Range Museum

875. Books that show military life from different perspectives
- *Humor in Uniform (Reader's Digest)*
- *Uncle John's Bathroom Reader Salutes the Armed Forces*
- *Battlefields and Blessings: Stories of Faith and Courage*

876. Military poems

"TO LUCASTA, GOING TO THE WARS"

Tell me not, sweet, I am unkind,
That from the Nunnery
Of thy chaste breast, and quiet mind,
To War and Arms I flee.

True, a new Mistress now I chase,
The first Foe in the Field;
And with a stronger Faith embrace
A Sword, a Horse, a Shield.

Yet this inconstancy is such
As you too shall adore;
I could not love thee, Dear, so much,
Loved I not Honor more.

–ROBERT LOVELACE

discipline is the word for these days
ignore the sand flea that just flew into your ear
biting and licking the blood
that should be feeding weakened muscle
how do I
express discipline
to people who have never seen it?

–JOHN SCHAEFFER,
U.S. Marine and coauthor of *Keeping Faith*

877. Military phrases that have entered our general vocabulary

Down the hatch—A drinking expression that originated in the Navy where cargoes were lowered down the hatch of the ship

End state—Set of conditions that need to be achieved to resolve the situation or mission

R&R (rest and recuperation)—Known to some as rest and recovery or more enticingly as rest and relaxation

Clean bill of health—Originated in the document issued a ship showing the port it sailed from had no epidemics or infection at time of departure

Flying by the seat of your pants—Deciding a course of action as you go along, using your own initiative and perceptions rather than a predetermined plan or mechanical aids. From early aviation parlance, when aircraft had few navigation aids and flying was accomplished by means of the pilot's judgment. The term emerged in the 1930s.

All present and accounted for—In the military, the response to a roll call is "all present or accounted for," meaning that everyone either is in formation or has a previously approved excuse. In the civilian world, the phrase has morphed to the redundant "all present and accounted for," which has come to mean "everyone is here" or even "we have all the equipment we need."

Rise and shine—Originally a military order from the late nineteenth century; now just as frequently used by a parent or a camp counselor with children

Spit and polish—Boot shining often did include "spitting" or adding water to polish to polish boots.Now used by the general population to describe a thorough cleaning.

Go ballistic—Originally referred to a guided missile going out of control; now refers to someone who suddenly becomes irrational or furious

Up in arms—A phrase from the sixteenth century, meaning to be in combat against an enemy; now used to mean being openly outraged about something

Gizmo—Originally U.S. Navy and Marine Corps slang, of unknown origin, used for a mechanical device or part that you didn't know the name of; used widely now in the civilian world for the same thing

878. **The sense of intense pride and patriotism you feel when you realize you're defending the very freedoms and country that influential musical artists sing about**

When Tim McGraw performed his song "If You're Reading This" as a tribute to fallen warriors at the 2007 Academy of Country Music Awards, there wasn't a dry eye in the house. We also tear up or at least feel our throats tighten every time we hear Lee Greenwood's "God Bless the USA" or Toby Keith's "Courtesy of the Red, White & Blue."

The power of music to move us to tears is not new. It is said that President Lincoln wept when he first heard the "Battle Hymn of the Republic."

List your favorite patriotic songs

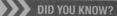

DID YOU KNOW?

> Thirty U.S. presidents served in the military.

879. Veterans

AIR FORCE

- **Heather Wilson**—first Air Force Academy graduate to be elected to U.S. Congress
- **Chuck Norris**—actor, martial arts champion
- **Robert F. McDermott**—USAA executive
- **George Steinbrenner**—baseball executive, businessman, former general's aide
- **Chesley Sullenberger**—U.S. Airways pilot who safely landed in Hudson River

ARMY

- **Alan Alda**—actor, director, screenwriter
- **Tony Bennett**—singer
- **Clint Eastwood**—actor, director
- **Jocelyn Elders**—U.S. Surgeon General
- **Malcolm Forbes**—publisher, philanthropist
- **James Earl Jones**—actor
- **Frank Joseph "Buster" Keaton**—actor, comedian
- **Rocky Marciano**—heavyweight boxing champion
- **Audie Murphy**—the most decorated soldier in World War II. Audie Murphy received every U.S. award, including the Medal of Honor. He not only received thirty-three medals from the United States but also received decorations from the Belgian and French armies. When he returned to the United States, he acted in more than forty movies until he was killed in a plane crash at the age of forty-six.
- **Andy Rooney**—CBS news broadcaster
- **Charles Schulz**—cartoonist

- **Gene Siskel**—movie critic
- **Dave Thomas**—founder and CEO of Wendy's
- **Charles Walgreen**—pharmacist, drug store chain owner, Illinois Volunteer Cavalry (Spanish-American War)

COAST GUARD

- **Sid Caesar**—actor
- **Jack Dempsey**—heavyweight boxing champion
- **Buddy Ebsen**—actor
- **Alex Haley**—author, *Roots: The Saga of an American Family*
- **Wycliffe "Bubba" Morton**—Major League Baseball player

MARINE CORPS

- **Leslie M. "Bud" Baker Jr.**—Chairman of the Board, Wachovia Bank
- **Patty Berg**—founding member, Ladies Professional Golf Assoc.
- **John Besh**—chef in New Orleans
- **Art Buchwald**—humorist
- **Drew Carey**—actor, comedian, host of *The Price Is Right*
- **Mike Farrell**—actor
- **John Glenn**—astronaut, senator
- **Gene Hackman**—actor
- **Brian Keith**—actor
- **Harvey Keitel**—actor
- **William Procter**—founder of Procter and Gamble
- **Shaggy**—Reggae/pop superstar
- **Fred W. Smith**—CEO of FedEx

NAVY

- **Johnny Carson**—host of *The Tonight Show*
- **Bill Cosby**—actor, comedian
- **R. Buckminster Fuller**—inventor, engineer
- **George Westinghouse**—inventor, engineer, businessman, Union Navy (Civil War)
- **Montel Williams**—talk show host, motivational speaker

880. Inspiring and accomplished military leaders

- Gen. Dwight D. Eisenhower
- Gen. Colin Powell
- Gen. Alexander Haig
- Gen. Douglas MacArthur
- Gen. George C. Marshall
- Gen. George S. Patton, Jr.
- Gen. Henry "Hap" Arnold
- Gen. John Pershing
- Gen. H. Norman Schwarzkopf
- Gen. Omar Bradley
- Vice Admiral James Stockdale
- Lt. Gen. Lewis Burwell "Chesty" Puller

*O beautiful for heroes prov'd
in liberating strife,
Who more than self their country lov'd
and mercy more than life*

–"America the Beautiful" by KATHLEEN LEE BATES

881. The ways that wounded warriors inspire all of us with their resiliency and accomplishments

Here's just one of many awe-inspiring stories:

In 2004 Staff Sgt. Jonathan Holsey was wounded while serving in Iraq and lost his leg. In 2009 he became the first amputee to graduate from the Army's Warrant Officer School.

In an interview with Army News Service, he reported that the instructors at the school showed him no favoritism because of his injury, and that the school was all-around challenging.

The Army warrant officer now frequently logs two to three miles per day to keep fit for military duty, and he's taken on activities he never attempted before, such as running a half-marathon. "When I first got injured, I thought if I could ever run again, I'd give it my all," he said.

Holsey plans to stay in the Army until he retires. "Because of the opportunities they've given us as wounded warriors," he told the Army News Service interviewer, "it's important for me to stay and help pave the way for others."

> *I'm a total civilian; I never served. When I was invited to join a group of other cartoonists to visit wounded warriors at Landstuhl Hospital in Germany, I didn't know what to expect. I expected depression, self-pity, negativity. What I found was the diametric opposite: unbelievable courage and positivity ... I watched them smile and laugh and tell us stories about home. We all came back so impressed with the caliber of the people defending our country.*
>
> –BILL AMEND, cartoonist, creator of *FoxTrot*

882. Military units helping the global community

In any given year, U.S. troops undertake humanitarian projects in nearly a hundred countries. Whether the emergency arises from an earthquake, hurricane, riot, flood, or forest fire, our military not only provides immediate and vital humanitarian relief (food and water, fuel, and communications equipment) but also conducts search-and-rescue and evacuation missions.

> *A thing to love: seeing a bright orange [Coast Guard] helicopter overhead when you need it most! Haiti, Katrina, Persian Gulf, Iraq ... the Coast Guard is worldwide and at every natural disaster, we arrive with hope.*
>
> –MIKE SMITH, retired U.S. Coast Guard Commander and Executive Director for the Coast Guard Festival in "Coast Guard City, USA"

883. Military Olympians

》》 DID YOU KNOW?

As part of the World Class Athlete Program, there have been 541 Army soldier-athletes selected since 1948 to an American summer or winter Olympic team, and they've earned 131 Olympic medals in a variety of sports from hockey and rowing to track and field, shooting, and boxing.

884. Benefiting from our Service members' uncommon courage, will, and standard of excellence when providing our nation's defense

A veteran is someone who, at one point in his life, wrote a blank check made payable to the United States of America for an amount of "up to and including my life."

–AUTHOR UNKNOWN

885. Our all-volunteer military

Less than one percent of the U.S. population serves in our military. In a time of war, what should that mean to the rest of us?

–KRISTIN HENDERSON, journalist, author, and Navy chaplain's spouse

886. Veteran-owned businesses—Buy Veteran!

887. Homeland and maritime security

888. Hospital ships

889. Liberty

It is easy to take liberty for granted, when you have never had it taken from you.

–AUTHOR UNKNOWN

890. Border patrol, antidrug task forces, forest firefighting

These and other missions connect the military with the country they serve.

891. Blue Star banners

Since World War I, Blue Star banners have been displayed by families, loved ones, and organizations to honor Service members on active duty during times of war.

Photo by Staff Sgt. Larry Reid Jr

892. Witnessing the extreme precision of the military

★ The thrilling performances of the Blue Angels, the U.S. Navy's Flight Demonstration Squadron, our country's oldest flying aerobatic team

★ The precise aerobatic formations of the Air Force Thunderbirds

★ The joy of watching a demonstration of the Army's Golden Knight Parachute Team falling from the sky while patriotic music is being played in the background

★ Admiring and appreciating members of the USMC Silent Drill Platoon as they execute a series of calculated drill movements while handling their hand-polished ten-and-a-half-pound M1 Garand rifles with fixed bayonets

★ Sitting on the beach at Ocean City watching a demonstration of incredible skills by the Coast Guard Search and Rescue Team

893. Bob Hope: The first and only honorary veteran of the U.S. Armed Forces
His first USO show was on May 6, 1941, at March Field, California.
He continued to travel and entertain troops for the rest of World
War II and later during the Korean War, the Vietnam War, the
third phase of the Lebanon Civil War, the latter years of the Iran-
Iraq War, and the 1990-1991 Persian Gulf War.

When overseas, he almost always performed in Army fatigues
as a show of support for his audience. Over the course of half a
century, he appeared in or hosted at least 199 USO shows.

For his service to his country, through the USO, he was
awarded the Sylvanus Thayer Award by the U.S. Military Academy at West Point in 1968.

When an act of Congress named Hope an "Honorary Veteran"
in 1997, he remarked, "I've been given many awards in my lifetime—but to be numbered among the men and women I admire
most—is the greatest honor I have ever received."

894. Understanding freedom isn't free
Eternal vigilance is the price of liberty.
–THOMAS JEFFERSON

>>> **DID YOU KNOW?**

There are 125,000 American military buried overseas in twenty-
four cemeteries created and maintained by the U.S. government,
through the American Battle Monuments Commission.

Photo by Kate Hartson

Marine Corps War Memorial (Iwo Jima)

Photo by Kate Hartson

HERE RESTS IN
HONORED GLORY
AN AMERICAN
SOLDIER
KNOWN BUT TO GOD

Tomb of the Unknown Soldier, Arlington, Va.

895. Memorials

Veterans memorials are found in towns and cities around the country. There are many national memorials, most of them in Washington, D.C., but in other locations as well.

But the freedom that they fought for, and the country grand they wrought for, is their monument to-day, and for aye.

–THOMAS DUNN ENGLISH

- **Korean War Veterans Memorial**
- **American Veterans Disabled for Life Memorial (new, to be finished November 2012)**
- **Women in Military Service for America Memorial**
- **Marine Corps War Memorial (Iwo Jima)**
- **Navy Memorial**
- **Air Force Memorial**
- **Vietnam Veterans Memorial (The Wall)**
- **National World War II Memorial**
- **Pearl Harbor Memorial**

Photo by Kate Hartson

Nurses in the field as depicted by The Vietnam Women's Memorial

Photo by Allison Chastain

★

For a lot of soldiers,
there are two kinds of people:
those who serve and those who expect to be served,
and those who serve are pretty noble.

–COL. DAN WILLIAMS,
helicopter brigade commander,
father of an Army 2nd lieutenant,
and spouse of a retired officer

★

WORTH STAYING FOR

─────※─────

Duty, Honor, Country—those three hallowed words
reverently dictate what you want to be,
what you can be, what you will be.

–GEN. DOUGLAS MACARTHUR

896. Getting to know people from all walks of life

Often becoming best friends with someone you might never have
interacted with in a nonmilitary life

> Let's celebrate the fact that we have the great opportunity to in-
> teract with such a diverse group of people. As Army spouse
> Theresa Donahoe says, "One thing I've learned in this lifestyle
> is to expand my definition of 'friend' in the military spouse arena.
> I had to learn that just because my initial impression of someone
> might be that they were 'not my type,' I often found that my
> 'type' was changing and that I enjoyed a much larger variety of
> friends than I ever had growing up. People I may never have
> given myself a chance to know in my old life turned out to be-
> come some of my closest and dearest friends." Those diverse
> friends help you to stretch and grow as you move through this
> life. We've found that there is a strong bond among military
> spouses—or at least there can be if you are open to it. We have
> all entered a life that is different and often difficult for all of us.

–KATHIE AND HOLLY, from *Help! I'm a Military Spouse. I Get a Life, Too!*

897. Service, selfless service, serving together for a common cause, or serving together for the greater good

My three years in the Marine Corps affected the way I viewed the world. Before I enlisted, I had no particular ethical orientation. I wanted to be cool, like Jim Morrison of the Doors, or Sean Penn's perpetually stoned surfer character Jeff Spicoli in *Fast Times at Ridgemont High*. I wore cutoff jeans and Rolling Stones T-shirts riddled with holes, skipped school to drink beer at an abandoned skateboard park, and managed to get kicked out of advanced placement math. If you had asked me to articulate my values, I would have been struck dumb. At best, I might have quoted Spicoli: "All I need are some tasty waves, a cool buzz, and I'm fine."

The Marines destroyed my prior character and rebuilt me in their own image. The impact was profound. I enlisted for selfish reasons: to travel, to have some adventures, and to get away from Houston. The idea of service to country was far from my mind. The Marines changed all that. Day in and day out, they taught me to believe that my country and my Corps were a higher priority than my own well-being and that some things are so important that they are worth dying for ... The intense training in the value of patriotism permanently influenced my values. Today I still think like a Marine. To me, the primary purpose of life is to serve others, not yourself, and to work to make the nation a better place.

–JOHN KROGER, attorney general of Oregon and former U.S. Marine

898. The feelings of pride, patriotism, and community that come from standing up for our national anthem before a movie starts
"The Star-Spangled Banner" is not just for sporting events when you're in the military!

899. Your twenty years of personal sacrifice net financial security
Allows you to pursue alternative careers, pleasurable pursuits, or important community programs

900. Going out to lunch and finding out someone anonymously picked up your check

901. Totally independent "dependents"

Real-life experience forces family members to become independent through situations they might not experience in civilian life, such as during deployments or when taking on leadership positions on the home front.

When another military spouse handed Marine spouse Mollie Gross a 1940 book with the comment "This will teach you to be a proper dependent," Mollie's response was, "Proper dependent!? With my husband gone all the time and me having to do everything by myself, I am anything but 'dependent'! I am my husband's 'INdependent'!"

I wake up to the reveille / Out of will that's all my own,
I've marched a twenty-mile hike, / And never left my home,
I've labored over haircuts, / Yet my hair is seldom groomed,
I've forgotten sweet sung melodies, / And now hum the Army tunes,
I've creased many uniforms, / The ones I never wear,
I've folded clothes for thee, GI, / With precision and tender care,
I've polished medals and spit shined boots, / That don't belong to me,
I've been kissed good-bye so many times, / And yet I never leave,
I've jumped out from an airplane, / And have never left the ground,
I've fired weapons and thrown grenades, / Yet never heard a sound,
I stood so straight on graduation, / As proud as I could be,
But heads were turned the other way, / And no one noticed me,
But it's ok I don't mind, / For it's my way of life,
You see I'm not a soldier, / I'm a soldier's wife.

–AUTHOR UNKNOWN,
  from a cross-stitched piece given to Tara by a dear family friend

902. Experiencing incredible personal growth, over and over and over again

Americans never quit.

–GEN. DOUGLAS MACARTHUR

903. Raising culturally aware children

You have the opportunity to open the world to your children, to really expand their horizons about other people, nations, and cultures.

904. Becoming culturally aware yourself

The commendable way the military celebrates diverse cultures with observances such as Hispanic Heritage Day or Asian Pacific Heritage Day

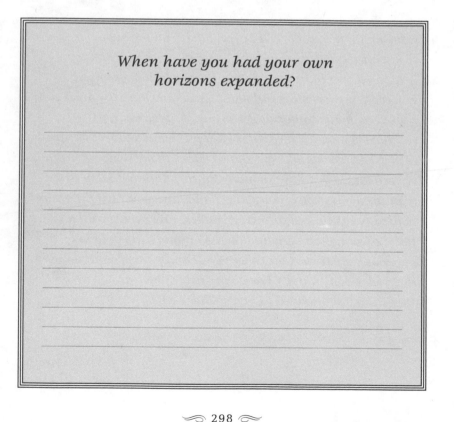

When have you had your own horizons expanded?

Photo by Mass Communication Specialist 2nd Class Casey H. Kyhl

905. Team-building training and experience

*Going to combat isn't about how strong you are,
it's about how strong we are. These aren't just your buddies
… these are your brothers.*

–ARMY STAFF SGT. SALVATORE "SAL" GIUNTA,
Medal of Honor recipient

Photo by 1st Lt. Darrick Noah

Battle buddies pull security during Operation Kherwar Pahtar, Kherwar District, Logar province, Afghanistan.

906. Battle buddies

907. The rewarding feeling that we're part of a legacy that predates the birth of our nation

Soldiers feel they owe something to those who came before them, and spouses serve from the home front just as wives have been the "home front" since ... forever.

908. "We do more before nine in the morning than most people do all day." It's true!

909. The feeling that you've done good work

When you get a phone call or a note from a younger Service member you've mentored saying what a difference you've made in his or her life

910. Community

The people in the military become your new family.
Doors are always open. Blood willing to be shed for
another is thicker than blood that runs through veins.

–MOLLIE GROSS, *Confessions of a Military Wife*

911. The ongoing adventure of this life

912. The social change and advancement that has often started in the military even before it does in civilian life

I realized that the military was the most level playing field that I could ever have imagined. Now, after decades of commercial airline flying and entrepreneurial business experience, I have yet to encounter an environment that compares ... [During military pilot training] it became clear. I understood that it was possible for a pilot's performance to be more significant than a pilot's gender. As time went on, I also came to understand that because of the seriousness of military missions, those involved focused on what was accomplished, rather than on the gender of who accomplished it.

–COLLEEN HENSLEY, author of *The Pilot—Learning Leadership,*
former Air Force pilot

I've had young Marines in Afghanistan read my book
[about the Vietnam War] and say, "Nothing has changed
except we don't have the racial tensions you all had back
then." I believe the military really is the institution where
the races first learned not to fear each other and to work
together. In the military you not only had to interact with
each other, you had to really rely on each other in life-and-
death situations. That makes a big difference.

–KARL MARLANTES, author of *Matterhorn,* a highly decorated
Marine Corps officer, and veteran of Vietnam

>>> **DID YOU KNOW?**

You can preserve personal and unit history through Remember My Service (RMS), an interactive service record with a DVD compilation of pictures, music, narration, video, and web links.

913. Military history and being a part of it

A few years ago my husband, Greg, was asked to do a presentation to the Japanese military on how ROTC and JROTC work in the U.S. Army. While there, his Japanese military escort took him to a military museum.

Greg found himself standing in front of a painting of Pearl Harbor, from the viewpoint inside the cockpit of a plane up above. Without realizing he was speaking out loud, Greg said what was in his mind, "My dad was in Pearl Harbor." The young Japanese major's eyes popped open wide. He didn't know what to say. Neither did Greg.

It's just one of the many times we've been struck by how the world changes and how much military members and their families live through so much of it, not just reading about it in newspapers or watching events on television.

My father was an Army sergeant who fought the Germans in WWII. Years later, married and with three kids, he ended up back in Berlin, Germany, working civil service for the U.S. Army. We all watched the Berlin Wall go up in 1961, experiencing life in a city surrounded by the Eastern bloc, fearful that the Russians might move in at any time.

Years later, in the Army myself, I crossed through Checkpoint Charlie into East Berlin. In those days, you had to sign in with a set time to return. If you didn't return by that time, there would be a search. You had to wear your uniform so you really stood out. It was an eerie feeling to tour East Berlin, hearing negative comments from some of the East Germans.

By that time we had so many West German friends. Greg's MP unit had a partnership with a German MP unit. We were invited to the wedding of the German MP commander who asked us to come in uniform. As we spent a long evening talking with his father and friends, we discovered many of them had been in the Waffen-SS during WWII, and some spent time in U.S. POW camps in the United States. Now here we were sipping champagne, mutually celebrating a wedding.

A few years after perestroika opened up relations between the United States and Russia, Greg and I were both attending a military leadership school. One day a group of Russian military personnel toured the school, learning how the U.S. Army trains its leaders. After so many years of fighting the Cold War, we all felt a bit odd at the sight.

Just one more reminder that relations with former enemies can normalize and improve over time. Good to know.

–KATHIE

914. Sacrifice

In each and every instance, we have been moved not just by your sacrifices, but by your incredible spirit and commitment to America.

–DR. JILL BIDEN, speaking about military members and their families

915. Career progression

The military has, for the most part, a pretty good promotion program. You know what you have to do to get promoted, and it's almost impossible to discriminate. It can happen but it's pretty hard to do.

916. The kindness of neighbors when they know your spouse is deployed

Mowing your lawn without being asked or running to the pharmacy when you're too sick to leave the house

917. When you finally understand fully that this is not a job ... this is "who your husband or wife really is" or who you really are: a military family

I have loved every minute and wouldn't trade with the wife of any other profession.

–JULIA COMPTON MOORE, Army wife and mother, advocate for military families during the Korean War and Vietnam War eras

918. Driving through the gate of any military installation and immediately having a sense of familiarity

919. "Lessons learned"

920. "Tools in your toolkit"

921. Being able to be an important part of America's Homeland Defense

922. Being well respected by your peers, your bosses, and those on your team

923. Experience working with a wide variety of people
From every part of our country and many parts of the world, from different socioeconomic backgrounds, and from many different ethnic backgrounds

924. Teamwork

I really never knew anyone in the military until I met Kathie and Greg. So I didn't really know anything about military training. But here's something I'll never forget. Kathie and I were taking a kayak rescue course ... what to do when your kayak flips. It was my turn and I was struggling to get myself back up into the boat. I didn't really have the arm strength. Kathie was leaning over the whole time, yelling encouragement, *"Come on Sarah, you can do it. You've almost got it. Just a little more. Come on. We know you can do it. Of course you can do it."* I'd never experienced that kind of team encouragement before—in anything. When I told this to Kathie later, after I had indeed made it into the boat, she looked at me in surprise. *"That's how we did everything in the Army ... helping each other out, encouraging each other. Of course."*

–SARAH RICHARDS, owner, Lavender Winds Farm,
Whidbey Island, Washington

Everything we are called upon to do in the Army requires teamwork, and teamwork is built on a foundation of trust and confidence within units—between Soldier and Soldier, between leaders and led, and between units who see themselves serving side by side. That trust and confidence emerges from our daily commitment to our Army values. Without trust, there can be no dignity and respect for the individual Soldier, and cohesion and morale in our units would suffer.

–GEN. ERIC K. SHINSEKI, former U.S. Army Chief of Staff

Navy photo by Petty Officer 1st Class Gregory Badger

Plebes paddle pontoon boats during a team-building portion of U.S. Naval Academy training.

925. Never a dull moment!

As military spouse Kris says, "It is so overwhelming at times, especially the moves, but as my Grandma used to say, 'I'll take the roller coaster over the carousel any day!' "

From *Help! I'm a Military Spouse: I Get a Life Too!*

926. Seeing examples of responsibility, discipline, respect, and professionalism

Every day all around you, in both military members and military spouses

927. The opportunity to make friends from so many different countries and cultures, nationwide and worldwide

928. Mentoring or "taking care of your own"

Because you've earned the right and know a thing or two

Two weeks after Ben joined the USCG they flew him to Cuba to meet the 721 for the first time. When he got to Cuba on that Friday, he discovered the boat wouldn't be there until Sunday. He wasn't able to access any of his money from Cuba and was without any way to eat or wash his clothes for the weekend. But, he met a woman who was in the USCG (higher rank than him) who was also waiting on the 721 and she took him under her wing that weekend. Also, he was given a sub sandwich by a lady who worked at the sub shop on the base. We were so grateful for those ladies. It's hard when they're away; you feel so helpless to their situations. But, it was nice to know that with the uniform came that automatic bond of brotherhood. And that God answered a mother's prayer across those many miles of ocean.

–THE WILEY FAMILY

929. Learned adaptability—resiliency

The incredible skill-building that is forced upon us by moves and deployments—as military members, military spouses, and military brats

The deployment of a parent in the Armed Forces is one of the most difficult things for a family member to go through. However, these trying periods when I was separated from my father ultimately helped me become the person I am today. Deployments can be a time of great personal sacrifice, but for me they became a time of great personal growth.

–JACK SHAFFIELD, Operation Purple Leadership Camp participant

Although deployments are very difficult while they are ongoing, they help me put life in perspective, and I think actually make my marriage stronger and my relationships with friends more special, and help me focus on what is really the important stuff in life.

–CATHY STERLING, Air Force brat, Army wife, advisor and mentor
to military families

Photo by Gertrud Zach, U.S. Army

930. True bravery

> *But, the bravest are surely those who have the clearest*
> *vision of what is before them, glory and danger alike,*
> *and yet notwithstanding, go out to meet it.*

–THUCYDIDES

931. The excitement of finding out that a good friend from an earlier assignment is being assigned to where you are currently stationed

932. Hope

What many military members will tell you is they believe they are giving their children a hope for the future ... taking the fight to the enemy rather than having the enemy and the fights come here to the United States.

> *I dream of giving birth to a child who will ask,*
> *"Mother, what was war?"*

–EVE MERRIAM, poet

933. Passion

Photo by Jessica LeAnn Daughtry

*There was an American girl,
who wanted to give life a whirl.
She married a soldier, to love and to hold her,
and wound up seeing the world.*

*That lucky girl became Army Wife,
who always stands proud no matter the strife.
She counts it a blessing and goes on professing,
"Nothing beats this passionate life."*

–STARLETT HENDERSON

934. "Serving" as a spouse and not even having to wear a uniform
How funny is it that as a spouse we say, "We were stationed ..."
or "We did flight training at ... " Obviously, spouses are not given
orders—not directly—but we sure follow them.

935. The quiet, friendly banter of a mid watch
Discussing happenings in ports already visited and expectations for those still to come

936. How "serving" as a spouse makes the heart swell with pride and gratitude at the mere sight of a uniform
"Hottie"—husband in uniform, Wow!
"Smokin'"—wife in uniform, Wow!

Photo by Staff Sgt. Michel Sauret

No long-distance calling necessary for this married couple who ended up deployed
to the same location.

937. The intense lifelong friendships and "surrogate families" that develop among the spouses of deployed Service members

938. Homesteading

939. Living "the Village" concept on installations

Where you co-parent your child with other parents or "take care of each other and our children"

940. Senior spouses

Especially the many who use their knowledge and experience to mentor others and push for changes important to all military families

941. The way officers straighten up when passing by the Sergeant Major, Master Chief, etc.

> *Whether supporting, training, or fighting,*
> *America looks to you to BE, KNOW,*
> *and DO what is right.*
>
> –GEN. ERIC K. SHINSEKI

942. Chief's Mess

943. Military ID

Don't leave home without it. Military ID cards give you access to every installation of any service.

944. Terms of endearment

Band of brothers

Silent ranks

Backbone of the military

Brotherhood

Sisterhood

Band of sisters

945. Understanding the concept of "mission first"

Sarah Hertig said her Army husband would prefer their daughter "never, ever" marry a soldier.

He'd rather spare her the roller coaster that's life as an Army wife, she said—the constant good-byes, the wartime fears, and the worry that seems to creep up every time there's an unexpected knock on the door.

But Hertig knows they can't predict who will sweep their daughter off her feet, as her soldier husband did with her. So she wrote her thirteen-year-old daughter a letter, just in case, to share the incredible highs and the heartbreaking lows of military life.

… She began her letter: "As much as I would like to tell you it is a life full of pride and patriotism, which it is, I feel I have an obligation to tell you about the hardships and realities that also come with this life."

In the letter, Hertig recalled the first time her husband went to war, when her daughter was five. She remembered watching her daughter as she walked with her father to his departure point, clutching his hand while she balanced his too-big helmet on her head.

Photo by Jessica LeAnn Daughtry

They were surrounded by families in tears, reluctantly saying good-bye to their military loved ones.

"I looked at you and you weren't crying," she said to her daughter. "And when it was time for you to say good-bye, you gave your dad his helmet, you hugged him around the neck, you kissed him, and you said, 'See you soon.' "

... If her daughter becomes an Army wife, she said, "there will be times you don't want to let go and you feel like you can't be brave ... but you don't have a choice."

At those times, her Army family will bolster her and she will bolster others, Hertig said, and those relationships will become her most treasured possessions.

... [After injuries kept him from the next two deployments], in 2009, Hertig's husband was cleared to deploy, and both felt at peace about his call to duty, she said.

Hertig and her daughter drove him to his unit as before, and when it was time to say good-bye, "You hugged your dad around his neck, you kissed him and said, 'See you soon.' "

He turned and walked away while Hertig's now twelve-year-old daughter stood there, stoically, bravely, staring after him in the night.

"Once again being brave for your dad," she said.

Loving a soldier isn't easy, Hertig said. "But things worth having in this life are never easy. By marrying a soldier you'll need to understand his job, his mission, his duty to country will always come first. By accepting that, I hope that you will learn to love this life as much as I do.

"I wouldn't trade it for the world," she added. "Not a moment."

–ELAINE WILSON-SANCHEZ, "Army Wife Shares Letter to Daughter at TEDxPentagon Event," American Forces Press Service, Nov. 19, 2010

946. Post- 9/11 GI Bill benefits that can be transferred to spouses or children

947. Financial security

Your guaranteed paycheck and steady job means knowing that your family will always be taken care of.

948. Bonuses
Enlistment, retention, and reclass incentives and re-enlistment bonuses

949. Special pay based on specialty or situation
Some examples:
- Hardship Duty Pay
- Hostile Fire/Imminent Danger Pay
- Aviation Career Incentive Pay
- Career Sea Pay, Diving Duty Pay
- Flight Pay, Jump Pay
- Foreign Language Pay
- Special Pay for Medical Officers
- Submarine Pay

What do you remind yourself is "worth it"
when reenlisting?

---

950. The Core Values

A life living out core values as timeless as our nation. They are a reminder of who we are, what it takes to get the mission done, and how to conduct ourselves both professionally and in our personal lives.

AIR FORCE
Integrity First, Service before Self, Excellence in All We Do

ARMY (Acronym: LDRSHIP for Leadership)
Loyalty, Duty, Respect, Selfless Service, Honor, Integrity, Personal Courage

COAST GUARD
Honor, Respect, Devotion to Duty

MARINE CORPS
Honor, Courage, Commitment

NAVY
Honor, Courage, Commitment

Photo by Petty Officer 2nd Class Andrew Meyers

Bill Cosby receives the Lone Sailor Award for veterans who have excelled in their civilian careers while exemplifying the Navy core values of honor, courage, and commitment.

951. The creeds we live by

Air Force Creed, Coast Guard Creed, Marine Creed, Navy Creed, Soldier's Creed. There are other creeds: Ranger Creed, Sapper Creed, NCO Creed

> "I am proud to be in the profession of arms," Sgt. Robert Wright told me as he waited for an airlift to Afghanistan. "When I came in I looked at it like a job, but now? I love saying the NCO Creed. It speaks for us, it's the standard we live by, what binds us as brothers and sisters in arms that you just can't get anywhere else."
>
> DAVID BOWNE WOOD, "In the 10th Year of War, a Harder Army, a More Distant America," Politics Daily, Sept. 9, 2010

952. The official service mottoes or slogans that encapsulate what we are all about

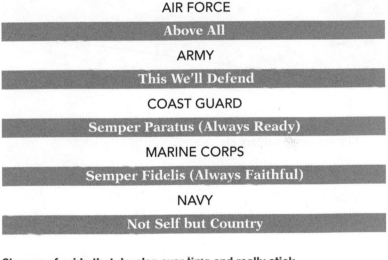

AIR FORCE

Above All

ARMY

This We'll Defend

COAST GUARD

Semper Paratus (Always Ready)

MARINE CORPS

Semper Fidelis (Always Faithful)

NAVY

Not Self but Country

953. Slogans of pride that develop over time and really stick

Once a Marine—Always a Marine

Warrior Ethos

Photo by Laura Fleming Photography

954. A lifetime of incredible memories, photos, and stories ... to share long after you leave military life

955. Senior Enlisted

Sergeant Major

"Gunny"

Master Chief Petty Officer

"Sea Daddy"

"Top"

Master Gunnery Sergeant

Chief Master Sergeant

"Chief of the Boat"

956. Feeling part of something bigger than yourself

957. Esprit de corps and camaraderie

> *There is no group of people with which I have come into
> contact—before or after my military service—of which
> I am more proud. The term "family" is frequently used, often
> inappropriately, when referring to a business organization.
> In the military, that term has true applicability. There is
> something about the bonds that form when everyone in
> your organization is willing to give his or her life for the
> stated mission.*

–COLLEEN HENSLEY

★

Character cannot be developed in ease and quiet.
Only through experience of trial and suffering
can the soul be strengthened, vision cleared,
ambition inspired, and success achieved.
–HELEN KELLER

★

REWARDS FOR
"LIVING THE LIFE"

≈≈≈ ★ ≈≈≈

We make a living by what we get,
but we make a life by what we give.

–WINSTON CHURCHILL

958. Development and demonstration of lifelong character

959. Friendships in the military that last a lifetime

960. Perspective

The sense of knowing what's really important in life that comes of having to leave your family to go to a war zone or of watching your spouse deploy into a war zone

> I think I first learned perspective—and to count my blessings—when my husband was deployed to Bosnia. He wasn't part of a U.S. Army unit deployment. He was one of the "onesies" pulled to participate in the U.N. Protection Forces, the "Blue Helmets." Whenever I heard President Clinton on the news saying we had no U.S. forces in Bosnia, I found myself yelling at the TV, "What's my husband then? Chopped liver? Doesn't he count?"
>
> With no Family Readiness Group or Rear Detachment Commander to turn to for information, and with no contact at all other than very erratic snail mail, I got my news of the war from that

"all-knowing source," CNN. I stayed glued to the International CNN News on our television in Bammental, Germany.

As I watched civilian deaths from snipings, people standing in long lines trying to get water for their families, and bombed-out homes—that minutes before looked a lot like the house I was currently living in—I found perspective in my life.

That lesson stayed with me. Now, very often, when I'm facing a challenge, I think as I take a shower in the morning, "Kathie, you don't have any real problems: you have hot running water, a roof over your head, plenty of food—and no one is shooting at you."

The hot shower has become a trigger for putting things in perspective. My life "as is" is far better than many people in this world will ever experience. I want to be grateful for what I already have rather than focus on what is missing.

Military families get lessons on perspective over and over again. When you watch your spouse deploy into a war zone, you come face to face with the reality that he or she might not return, or might not return whole. While other Americans might be able to simply go on with life as usual during a war, you can't. Your perspective on life necessarily turns to what is most important, to those truly important things you could so easily lose.

–KATHIE

961. The chance to leave a legacy

962. Military job fairs

963. Medical coverage in retirement
One of the biggest out-of-pocket expenses in retirement for most people

964. Free career and business training as well as resume/job search training
Through ACAP and Family Service Centers—programs that would cost you a lot in the civilian world

965. Payment for unused leave

966. Retirement pay

Sgt. Maj. William E. Thom II salutes during his retirement ceremony after more than thirty years of honorable service in the Marine Corps.

967. Sharing the bittersweet aspects of closing out a military life at retirement

I admit I'd been looking forward to this time in a way—to cleaning out my military closet—creating space in my life, both literally and figuratively. But it wasn't as easy as I expected.

I won't even try to describe the emotional and identity aspects of a military retirement. That would take a book in itself. Let's just look at the uniform aspects.

What do I do with all these perfectly good uniforms?

Like this perfectly good pot hat, one that I spent a good $60 or more on, that I hardly ever wore—do I just throw it in the trash? Taking it to the thrift shop to sell for a few dollars would have been hard enough but at least it would have gone on to a useful life. But it's no longer a valid uniform item.

What about the dress blues? Will I ever want to wear them again, and if so, would they still fit? Actually, they already don't fit that well anymore. Got to go. But where, to whom? With all the uniform changes I don't even have the satisfaction of giving these uniforms to younger military members, as Greg's ROTC professor passed on uniforms to Greg when he started his military career.

We tried the local community theater. Guess they've had many of these requests already and have no need for more. Plus not too many plays about the military.

I'll never use this purse in civilian life. It's gotta go. Ditto these shoes. Anyone who served would know I was wearing old uniform items with civilian clothes. It's just not done! And quite frankly, not my current style.

It seems a crime to throw away these boots—especially my WAC boots that I've hung onto and moved twenty times in the last thirty years. They haven't been authorized to wear for more years than I like to count, but they remain the most comfortable military boots I've ever owned—and part of my history.

I decide to plant the boots in our garden, and fill them with succulents. We live in the Northwest. With the weather here, I'm sure they will eventually dissolve and fade into the ground.

Maybe by then I'll be ready to clear out the rest of this closet.

–KATHIE

968. The possibility of turning your military experience into a follow-on career after the military

- Spouses to Teachers
- Troops to Teachers
- Helmets to Hardhats
- Military to Medicine and Heroes to Healthcare
- Combat Boots to Cowboy Boots

Following retirement from the military, many people step into careers that closely mirror what they did in the military. Military public affairs personnel start work in civilian media; military truck drivers start doing long hauls across the country for civilian firms; many individuals walk into very similar work as contractors. Still others find ways to creatively use their military experience and interests in totally new endeavors.

After a career with the U.S. Army, specializing in national security issues, counterterrorism, and counterinsurgency operations, Frederick J. Chiaventone channeled his military experience and love of military history into writing, as a novelist, historian, and screenwriter. He followed his award-winning novel, *A Road We Do Not Know*, about the Battle of the Little Bighorn, with other books, and was historical advisor to several film and television productions and subject matter expert in productions for PBS and the History Channel.

Linda and Gordon Thompson retired from the Pentagon after twenty- and twenty-one-year Army careers. They turned the experience they'd gained in people management, administration, protocol, logistics, planning, and team building into restructuring a successful small business, event, and destination management company in San Francisco. Cappa and Graham puts on large special events and meetings for corporate and association clients from around the world, handling themes, coordination, and transportation. From the Virgin Airlines Launch to a Levi Strauss Teambuilding for Charity event, they handle the details, just like a well-planned and -executed military campaign.

969. Veterans' preference

970. VA Home Loan Guaranty Program

971. Army and Navy Credentialing Opportunities Online (COOL)

COOL allows Service members to get civilian credentials to match their military occupational specialty.

See more at https://www.cool.army.mil or navy.mil.

972. A resume that makes you more competitive than career DoD civilians

973. A worldly Rolodex for life

974. Reminiscing about how much things change over time

Ask any veteran about the changes they saw during their military service and the changes they've seen in the military since they retired, and you'll start a lively conversation. Heck, ask anyone currently serving in the military who's been in a few years and they'll easily rattle off a list of changes.

Field food always triggers memories: "I remember C-rations in cans still being used when we started training ... They were probably using up old stock. Remember, they included cigarettes back then for our 'Smoke 'em if you've got 'em' training breaks. Now it's M&Ms in the MREs, Tobacco Cessation Classes, and designated smoking areas. And now they're talking about a total ban on smoking in the military!"

Bring up PT and open up comments:

"Hey, I remember when it was all side straddle hops and shuttle runs. Then it was sit-ups, push-ups, and the two-mile run. Now they are changing it again, to combat readiness test with things like running with a weapon, vaulting, crawling, a casualty drag, and sprints. Much more realistic to war, I'd say. Train like you'll fight ... and test like you'll fight."

We could go on and on about vehicle, equipment, and weapons changes: from five-ton and two-and-a-half-ton trucks to FMTVs, from Jeeps to Humvees to LTVs, from pack mules to robodogs. It's amazing we still have the M16.

And of course, the bigger changes. "Your reference point for when the world changed is 9/11," says one soldier. "It's our common denominator if you were on active duty. That's the day the world for the military started anew."

That was then ... this is now!
How have things changed?

975. Patriot Express loans

The U.S. Small Business Administration's Patriot Express Pilot Loan Initiative has supported nearly $500 million in six thousand Patriot Express loans over the course of three years to small businesses owned and operated by veterans, Reserve Service members, and their spouses.

Loans of up to $500,000 can be used for most business purposes. These have an enhanced guaranty and interest rate, and feature one of SBA's fastest turnaround times for loan approvals.

Patriot Express is available to military community members including veterans, Service-disabled veterans, active-duty Service members participating in the military's Transition Assistance Program, Reservists and National Guard members, current spouses of any of the above, and widowed spouses of Service members or veterans who died during service or of a Service-connected disability.

See more at www.sba.gov/patriotexpress.

976. Legacy families

I grew up in the Army and came from a family who, since 1862, has defended our nation. My great-grandfather, my grandfather, my father, my brother, my sister, my niece, and my husband are all veterans of this country's wars. My father is a veteran of three wars and is one of the twenty-five million veterans living today who served the nation with such incredible courage.

While I joined the Army right out of college, I planned to only stay in the Army to complete my two-year commitment, but it wasn't too long before I realized that there are no other shoes [boots] I would rather fill than the ones I am wearing right now. As a soldier you can continually serve. It is a calling to be a soldier and there is a great sense of pride and camaraderie in serving the greatest Army in the world.

–GEN. ANN E. DUNWOODY, first female four-star general in the U.S. military

Photo by Sgt. Jennifer Poole

Col. Jessie Farrington, 1st Combat Aviation Brigade commander, promotes his son, Christopher, to the rank of sergeant.

>>> **DID YOU KNOW?**

Holly Petraeus, head of the Office of Servicemember Affairs in the Consumer Financial Protection Bureau of the Department of Defense, is part of a military legacy family. Her son, brother, father, grandfather, and great-grandfather all served. Her husband, Gen. David H. Petraeus, former commander of U.S. and NATO forces in Afghanistan, retired from the U.S. Army in September 2011, after thirty-seven years of service, to become Director of the Central Intelligence Agency.

977. United Services Military Apprenticeship Program
Enlisted members of Navy and Marine Corps can apply their training and work experience toward a civilian journeyman certificate.

978. VA hospitals

979. Veterans disability benefits
Cash, education, competitive advantage

980. The Caregivers and Veterans Omnibus Health Services Act of 2010
To provide caregivers of Iraq and Afghanistan vets a living stipend, health coverage, support, and counseling

981. Patriot Guard Riders—"Standing for Those Who Stood for Us"

982. The National Anthem
The feeling of pride and connection that comes from watching civilians stand at attention during the national anthem and knowing, from their stance, that they are prior military

983. The many retired military and their spouses who volunteer at USO
Knowing how much that service means to young military members and their families

984. Giving old uniforms to teenagers and young adults in your neighborhood
Especially fatigues/BDUs with the tags off. They can be "cool," which sort of makes you "cool" in their eyes.

985. The instant camaraderie you have with the student veterans organization if you go back to school

986. Making your "dream sheet" with best military places to retire
Courtesy of Sperling's Best Places, USAA, and Military.com

987. Reunions
Veteran reunions and military unit reunions

You Know You Are a Veteran When ...
You wear a baseball cap with your ship's
name, even though the last time you
stepped on that ship was forty years ago

988. Military retirement communities
Continuing care retirement communities in locations all over the
country (but most often near military bases and military hospitals) that cater to former military members and their families

**989. Programs that keep you connected with the military and up to date on
your retirement benefits and any changes**

- **U.S. Air Force Retiree Services**
  www.retirees.af.mil

- **U.S. Army Retirement Services**
  www.armyg1.army.mil/retirees.asp

- **Marine for Life**
  A Marine Corps organization providing nationwide
  assistance to Marines returning to civilian life, Reserve
  Marines, and all Marine veterans throughout their lives.
  Marine for Life also assists Sailors who have served with
  Marine Corps units.

- **U.S. Navy Retired Activities Branch**
  www.public.navy.mil/bupers-npc/support/ retired_activities/
  Pages/default.aspx

- **U.S. Coast Guard Retiree and Annuitant Services Branch**

- **Retiree Appreciation Days and Military Retiree Seminars**
  Offered at many base/posts once a year to show
  appreciation for military retirees and their families and to
  give them current information about benefits, entitlements,
  health care, and special services available for them

Photo by Seaman Matthew Ebarb

990. Taking care of our own—burial benefits and traditions

The right to be buried in a military cemetery or at sea, one of the oldest traditions in naval history. There are few things as touching as a military funeral where "Taps" and the twenty-one-gun salute are rendered.

Blue sky overhead. Green leaves flutter in the Oklahoma breeze, and birds sing in the trees. Spring is here at last.

Newly turned red earth marks the place where one man will rejoin it. After traveling around the world, he returns to be buried surrounded by stones bearing familiar names.

Blue uniforms. Six men in formation approach the place, carrying a polished wooden box and a flag.

Family and friends reach out for a nearby hand, holding back sobs. They watch with pride, heads lifted high, refusing to be overcome with grief or miss one moment of the honor due their loved one. It is a ceremony he would be proud to see, and they silently hope he does see it from the burning blue, the sanctity of space he now shares with God.

The honor guard folds the flag in silence, broken only by muted commands and the trill of a bird. One Airman approaches the family and looks directly into the eyes of the widow:

"On behalf of the President of the United States, please accept this flag as a symbol of your loved one's honored and faithful service to this country."

Three times the rifles sound, and then the bugle plays "Taps." Day is done in the middle of a sunny afternoon.

Day is done for one veteran. One among millions who have served, lived, and died. Each is loved, mourned, and missed— during the funeral and for long afterward.

The ceremony is repeated often and sometimes too early for Soldiers, Sailors, Airmen, and Marines. Some die in service and some live to retire, but they all surrender their lives for love of country and belief in the flag that will eventually be extended over their caskets and offered to their next of kin.

I live on the home front. I've never experienced danger in the air or on a field of battle. But I've been on the front lines at the graveside of one who did, my father.

–TERRI BARNES, Air Force spouse and *Spouse Calls* blog columnist

991. Insurance and financial services specifically focused on the military and their families

- Pentagon Federal Credit Union
- NavyArmy Federal Credit Union
- Andrews Federal Credit Union
- Navy Federal Credit Union
- Armed Forces Insurance
- Armed Forces Bank
- USAA

  USAA is a prime example of military members stepping up to take care of their own. In the 1920s, Army officers experienced discrimination from insurance companies that thought their transient lifestyles made for a bad risk. Maj. William Henry Garrison gathered twenty-four of his fellow officers to discuss solutions, resulting in the formation of a mutual company, whereby they insured one another.

  USAA—United States Army Automobile Association— was incorporated in 1922. Over the years, it expanded its membership eligibility to include all members of the U.S. Armed Forces, active duty, Guard and Reserve, as well as those retired or honorably separated in the past, regardless of dates or branch of service, as well as their family members.

  Today, USAA has 22,000 employees and eight million members. Their mission has expanded well past auto insurance over time to provide a full range of highly competitive financial products and services striving to be the provider of choice for the military community.

DID YOU KNOW?

USAA is consistently ranked first in customer service, earning recognition from MSN Money Customer Service Hall of Fame and *Bloomberg Businessweek*, among others.

992. Programs that veterans or civilians create to thank our military members and veterans for their service in a tangible way

- **Veteran Tickets Foundation**
  www.vettix.org
  A nonprofit created by veterans to help citizens thank those who serve or have served. They gather donations of event tickets to pass on to military members and their families. As of early 2011, more than 171,000 tickets had been given out in forty-five states to active-duty military, veterans, and their families.

- **Thanks-A-Bunch**
  www.thanksabunch.org
  Sometimes schedules don't always allow Americans to simply sit down with one of America's Heroes and have lunch together. Thanks-A-Bunch (TAB) was created so anyone can present a card valued at $50 to an American Hero whenever or wherever they come into contact. For a tax-deductible contribution of only $10 you can give a gift that's convenient for America's Heroes to use any time at more than 18,000 participating restaurants across the country.

993. Department of Veterans Affairs

Our system of assistance for veterans has roots going back to 1636, when the Pilgrims of Plymouth Colony, who were at war with the Pequot Indians, passed a law stating that disabled soldiers would be supported by the colony. In 1930, three different Federal agencies became bureaus within the new Veterans Administration. In 1989, the Department of Veterans Affairs (VA) was established as a Cabinet-level position. "There is only one place for the veterans of America," said President George H.W. Bush, "in the Cabinet Room, at the table with the President of the United States of America."

> *To care for him who shall have borne the battle, and for his widow, and his orphan.*
>
> –ABRAHAM LINCOLN

994. Military associations and family associations
And the work they do to increase and protect our
hard-earned military benefits

- Military Officers Association
- Association of the United States Army
- Non-Commissioned Officers Association
- Reserve Officers Association
- American Legion and American Legion Auxiliary
- Veterans of Foreign Wars
- Disabled American Veterans
- National Military Family Association
- Blue Star Families
- National Guard Association
- Military Order of the Purple Heart
- National Veterans Association
- Legion of Valor
- American Retirees Association
- Air Force Association
- Air Force Sergeants Association
- Military Academy Alumni

**995. The chance to explore different parts of this country and world, then
decide where we would most want to live, all on Uncle Sam's dime**

> *In the Coast Guard, you can get to see most of the coastal
> United States during a career and discover amazing cities
> and towns you wouldn't have known about otherwise.*

–ROBERT GREEN, Lieutenant, U.S. Coast Guard, 1998-2004,
owner of CutterAgent Design and Services

- Special Forces Association
- Fleet Reserve Association
- Marine Corps League
- Association of Naval Aviators
- Naval Enlisted Reserve Association
- The Navy League
- Navy Reserve Association
- Submarine Veterans
- U.S. Naval Institute
- Women Marines Association
- The Military Coalition
- The Retired Officers Association (TROA)
- United Armed Forces Association
- National Association for Uniformed Services (NAUS)

Our members answered the call to serve our country in uniform. They protected our freedom, they earned their benefits through years of sacrifice and yes, even their blood, and they deserve our respect and our thanks. They also deserve to have the promises made to them by our government honored, just as they have honored America.

–WWW.NAUS.ORG

996. The ability to create community wherever you move in retirement because you've had to do that over and over in this military life

I interviewed a couple who spent seven years living on a sailboat. They raved about the sailing community.

"Living on a sailboat, it's easier to meet people than in land communities," said Renate. "It's very common to just head over to someone's boat in your dinghy—uninvited—to say 'Hi and welcome to port.' We always had spontaneous potlucks and get-togethers. I guess it's because you have like-minded people from all over the world with this instant camaraderie because we've all endured the same hardships."

"Sort of like military communities," I said.

"Exactly!" replied Renate. Her husband Dan nodded his head in agreement. Dan retired from the Army after twenty-plus years before they decided to try the sailing life.

When I wrote a column in the *Army Times* newspaper for many years, I often heard from readers about this topic, especially from those who had left the military community.

"It's a life—not a job," wrote one retired soldier. "If you live with other military families, you share the same problems, separation, low pay, constant moves, etc. There is closeness when trouble strikes." He went on to describe how different it was for him and his wife in the civilian world, how hard it was to get involved and to be accepted, to be included. He described how his daughter and son-in-law, who both left the Air Force after many years, find they miss the built-in community they always had in the service. "No one calls to ask for help," his daughter told him.

Now, years later, living in a nonmilitary area myself, I have seen the difference. Once we leave the familiar commonalities of military life, we have to work harder to get involved with the community around us. At first look that may seem difficult for military families, accustomed as they are to that instant, easy connection.

But I believe it's precisely the skills and habits of military life—learning to make new friends quickly, reaching out to others more automatically, stepping in to help, entertaining frequently—that equip us for community building. Plus, we've learned how important and wonderful a close-knit community can be.

–KATHIE

997. Making a difference and knowing it

My responsibility, our responsibility as lucky Americans, is to try to give back to this country as much as it has given us, as we continue our American journey together.

–GEN. COLIN POWELL

You Know You Are a Veteran When ...

You automatically stand at attention and get ready to salute when you see the color guard coming by in a parade, even when no one around you is bothering to stand up

You attend large air shows and look and point at the different planes saying, "Flown that, flown that one too, yup that one—oh, not that one"

You are drawn to read every obituary listing where the photo is obviously a service photo from long ago

You still find yourself automatically using Sir or Ma'am

You still automatically use the terms like latrine or head, roger that, and recon, even years after serving

Seeing someone with military plates or apparel means you are instant friends

You are watching a movie in a theater and the military aircraft in the movie are flying in a way that doesn't make sense and you get frustrated and blurt out, "That's not possible!"

A twenty-one-gun salute shakes your boots and brings on pride and tears

998. Identifying with other military veterans

999. The instant connection and shared history you feel when you meet another veteran

1000. The depth of relationship with your spouse and family, cultivated through years of challenge and constant separations and reunions

Photo by Stephanie Himel-Nelson

1001. Yankee Oscar Uniform

You got it!
One of the things to
love about military life is

Y-O-U.

ABOUT THE AUTHORS

 **Tara Crooks** is a thirteen-year military spouse known for her ability to inspire and empower. Tara holds a Bachelor of Business Administration in Human Resource Management, though she will smirk at its applicability to what she feels she was "born to do." Tara found her niche in starting *Army Wife Talk Radio* during her husband's first deployment in 2005. What began as a fun "hobby" grew in popularity as Tara realized that her experiences and need for resources were shared by many other military spouses.

Called "Oprah of the Armed Forces" by Katie Couric, Tara has been a featured military family life expert in *USAA Magazine, Military Times, Stars and Stripes*, Lifetime.com, Army.com, and Military.com and is a contributor to the *Household Baggage Handlers* book of military spouse stories.

She was named the American Legion Auxiliary Woman of the Year 2008 for her service to military families, and to *Who's Who among Military Spouses 2009* by *Military Spouse* magazine.

Tara has taken an active role in supporting her local military communities as an avid volunteer, Master Trainer, FRG leader, and Spouse Club board member. She has keynoted events such as AAFES Military Spouse Appreciation Day, Command and General Staff College Spouse Night, and U.S. Army Reserve Senior Leaders conference. In April 2011, Tara joined USAA as a Community Manager of their Military Spouse Community.

She and her husband, Kevin, have two daughters, two dogs, and a cat.

Starlett Henderson is a military veteran and National Guard spouse of sixteen years. She has her master's degree in Counseling. Her desire to counsel and uplift military families drives her as Army Wife Network's cofounder, speaker, and talk radio host.

Star has devotionals published in the most recent edition of the Battlefield and Blessing series, *Stories of Strength and Courage from the Wars in Iraq and Afghanistan.* She was awarded the FINRA Education Foundation's 2011 Military Spouse Fellowship, which provides training to earn the Accredited Financial Counselor® (AFC®) designation.

Star and her husband have two children.

Tara and Star teamed up in 2006 to publish "Field Problems," a military lifestyle Q&A column, and in 2007 began their spouse conference series Field Exercise. The pair founded Army Wife Network in 2009 to combine their radio show, column, conferences, and *Loving a Soldier* blog, providing interactive empowerment for Army wives by incorporating the power of social media.

★

Kathie Hightower is a military spouse of thirty-two years. Her Bachelor of Arts in German didn't lead to her current work, but the language sure helped her while she was stationed in Germany in the military and as she's traveled Europe presenting workshops for spouses.

An author, columnist, and international speaker, Kathie designs inspirational programs that encourage corporate and military audiences to access possibilities and "Jump Into Life." She's been called the "Dr. Phil of military spouses."

Besides the many columns coauthored with Holly Scherer that are listed below, Kathie has had frequent articles in R&R magazine, *Off Duty*, *Stars and Stripes*, and various post newspapers, along with many civilian publications. She is a contributor to *Household Baggage Handlers, Heart of a Military Woman*, and a number of nonmilitary books.

She is a retired lieutenant colonel from the Army Reserves; her husband is retired Army.

Holly Scherer is a military spouse of twenty-seven years. She has her master's degree in Human Development and Family Relations. She's also an author, columnist, and international speaker encouraging and enabling her audiences to live life "Now, not When."

In addition to her work in education and research, Holly has always been an active volunteer in her military community. She has received numerous awards for her contributions to military families worldwide, including Volunteer of the Year, Outstanding Civilian Service Medal from the Department of Defense, Commander's Award for Public Service, and the Army Engineer Association's prestigious *Essayons* Award.

She was cofounder and facilitator of the "People Encouraging People" welcome program for newcomers to Germany at her local military community, a program that became a blueprint for other military communities throughout Europe.

Her husband is retired military; they have two children and a dog.

Kathie and Holly have partnered in writing and workshops for military spouses of all services since 1994. They've presented their trademark workshop Follow Your Dreams While You Follow the Military for military spouses all over the United States, Europe, Japan, and Korea. They've keynoted many of the military spouse conferences of all services worldwide. Frequent contributors to military publications, including years of columns in *Air Force/Army/Marine Corps/Navy Times* newspapers, *Military Money* magazine, *Military Spouse* magazine, and Military.com, they are also coauthors of *Help! I'm a Military Spouse—I Get a Life Too!*, in its second edition. They were designated two of the first *Who's Who in Military Spouses 2007* named by *Military Spouse* magazine.

ACKNOWLEDGMENTS | From the four of us

We have so many people to thank for making this book happen. Some read through entire rough drafts ... that's going above and beyond!

Thanks to

Chip MacGregor and Amanda Luedeke with MacGregor Literary Agency, without whom we'd still be sending proposals to publishers.

Kate Hartson, our editor at Hachette. Talk about taking on a challenge ... effectively editing a book written in a language you don't speak!

Our packager, Roberta Conlan, for asking questions that made us get clearer in our writing.

Our copy editor, Julia Duncan, for the patience it takes to do this kind of detail work and fact checking.

Tina Taylor, book designer extraordinaire ... and an Army brat herself.

The art department for creating a book cover we all responded to with a "Hooah!"

The military cartoonists and artists who shared their work, adding the perfect touch.

The many military and military spouse photographers who contributed to this book. Who better than photographers who live the life to capture "real life" insider views? A special thanks to Laura Fleming, professional photographer and military spouse, who managed to take photos we needed in the midst of a move with her four children while her spouse was deployed.

And thanks to the many friends who read the book to give us Service-specific feedback, stories, and examples: Robert and Jocelyn Green, Mike and Vivian Greentree, the Kissinger family, Madonna Kramer, Mike Smith, the Wiley family, Terri Barnes, retired Colonel Guy C. Beougher, Wendy Poling, and Melissa Seligman.

★

From Tara

Thanks to my soldier, Maj. Kevin Crooks. What an incredible journey. You're my lobster!

Wrena and Chloe, you are the most amazingly resilient little girls. You are so loved.

Grandpa and Grandma, you taught me that every dream is possible, if you work hard enough. Thank you for believing in me. Even though you are no longer living, I still feel your presence.

Mama, Scott, Bill, and Jane—and our extended family—for your love and support.

Abbey and David Vogt—I treasure your friendship and respect of our family and all military families. You keep me grounded and "home" when I'm swept away.

Our military family—Many have left an indelible footprint on my heart as we've crossed paths on this journey.

The Penfield family and retired Command Sgt. Maj. Callaghan—for amazing mentorship that taught us the building blocks to a successful life in the military.

The Ford, Nauman, Tymochko, Ikena, and Silvers families and Mrs. Jamie Rubrecht—the "firsts" in our journey I'll never forget.

The Pardo and McTague families—for allowing me the joy of leading a successful Family Readiness Group.

The Rogers family—an entire family who never met a stranger.

The Mills, Flatebo, Cediel, and Varga families—the Lancaster Way crew! Incredible friendships and oh the memories!

The Norris, Culver, and Demasi families—Sill would have never been the same.

A special "Hooah" to Michael Kelly of USAA for believing in me even when I didn't believe in myself.

The Army Wife Network Team—You saw a need and you filled it. I am so thankful for your passion for military families and your unbelievably generous hearts.

★

From Starlett

Thanks be to God for guiding me to join the Army and this project.

Thanks to my husband and children—David, Thomas, and Tara—for not hearing or saying, "I can't" or "We can't." *To infinity and beyond!*

Thanks to my family. I am grateful to my father, William Green, and the Green family for their service and for passing the flame to me and my brothers—Will and Justin.

And to the Samuelsons led by my mother, Jo Samuelson, and Hendersons, Ray and Mary, for being faithful in their love and support from the home front.

I. N. D. I., I deeply appreciate you loving us all, through it all.

The "units" I've served with—the *Copper Kings, Arctic Warriors,* 103d, GAARNG, and Army Wife Network—represent for me a host of individuals I am better for knowing and serving with.

For inspiring or joining me, I'd like to thank Karl, Mick, J.T., Sara, the Gilje and Weinert families, Erin, Leah, and Mandy; you're my chosen military family. Thank you all.

I will not forget Paul Johnson, who serves still, as an emblem of patriotism and love for this country.

To Tara, Kathie, and Holly: I constantly meet spouses who tell me you've touched their lives and gotten them excited to follow their dreams. I'm thankful to all three of you for touching my life.

Finally, I have friends to whom I'm personally indebted for their support of me and my "troops."

Hugs to the Clifton, Davis, Hendrix, Luke, Malone, Poe, Schultz, Scott, Smith, and Weaver families, Nicki, Tamsen, Debbie, and Jenny.

It wouldn't be a life we love, without the people we love.

★

From Kathie

I was able to thank so many people in our first book, the oh-so-many friends and family members who've helped and inspired me during thirty years and twenty moves with the military. I won't repeat that long list here. You know who you are.

To my father, Joe Hotter, uncles Sam Walkama and Iggy Tenzyk, father-in-law Jack Hightower, and brother-in-law Gene Inzer—for their examples of stepping up to serve in time of war. And to Mom and Dad for encouraging me to serve ... wish you were still here to read this book.

To Holly, the perfect example of lifelong friends we so often make in military life—yes, we'll someday be those older retired friends enjoying vacations together at the Hale Koa. These years of workshops and writing together have been quite a ride. Here's to many more workshop and book-signing trips together. To Star, for keeping track of the many ideas and versions of this book. You're the Excel spreadsheet guru and researcher with a great sense of humor to boot. To Tara, our photo and social media diva. It's been great collaborating with like-minded people, focused on celebrating and supporting military members and their families.

My biggest thanks go to my husband, Greg. He kept me fed with gourmet meals and handled all the household tasks while I birthed this book. His humor and calm nature kept me from imploding when deadlines got crazy and my computer tried to die on me. Line item #315 definitely applies to me: "For some of us, it's where we met our spouse, and that's one really great thing to love about the military!"

★

From Holly

If you were meant to do things all by yourself, you would have been put here on this earth all by yourself.

The encouragement and love I've received from family, friends, and other amazing military spouses have allowed me to embrace this roller coaster ride of military life. A life I wouldn't change for anything because of the treasured friendships I've made and the person I've become as a result of the joys and challenges of military life.

My father died while we were writing this book, and my sister, Katie Bigus, was my Rock during those difficult months of grieving. Because of Katie, I came out on the other side of grief with a renewed sense of life, along with the passion and energy for this book.

Thank you to my brothers, Brad and Alan, and my stepmother, Ginny, for becoming my biggest cheerleaders in the absence of Dad. You're a true testament of what a loving family is all about.

Thank you to Tara, Star, and Kathie for all the hard work and, more important, for your friendship.

A special thank you to the Boatner, Buxbaum, Connett, Odierno, Rhoades, Riley, Rooney, Shibusawa, Sterling, and Winzenried families for your dedicated service to our country and for sharing your thoughts and stories in this book.

This wild ride wouldn't have happened without falling in love with the most ethical, brilliant, and handsome man I have ever met. I love you, Jack!

My children, Helen and Jack—what can I say? You both are amazing. I pray you will continue to use your strengths for the greater good, one of the keys to true happiness in life.

★

PHOTO SOURCES

The photos on the following pages are from DVIDS (Defense Video & Imagery Distribution System), www.dvidshub.net. Photographers are credited on their respective photos, when names are available.

p. 24, 33, 36, 41, 45, 79, 104, 108, 152, 155, 165, 173, 189, 201, 206, 213, 215, 217, 220, 222, 224, 227, 228, 229, 234, 239, 241, 242, 251, 255, 257, 260, 267, 280, 289, 300, 305, 309, 314, 318, 321, 327, 330

The photos on the following pages are from Defense Visual Information (DVI) Directorate, www.DefenseImagery.mil. Photographers are credited on their respective photos, when names are available.

p. 61, 63, 299, 307

Other sources:

p. 6—PD-USGov-Military-Army; p. 17—PD-USGov-Military-Air Force; p. 18—PD-USGov-Military-Navy; p. 65—USAG Schweinfurt Public Affairs; p. 71—Exchange Public Affairs; p. 124—iCreative Media - A division of Semo Media LLC

CREDITS AND PERMISSIONS

Worth Joining For

p. 14, Scott Dietrich—reprinted with permission. *I'm Big in Japan* Blog, http://afscottd.blogspot.com.

p. 14, Eldonna Lewis Fernandez—reprinted with permission. Sheryl Roush and Eldonna Lewis Fernandez, *Heart of a Military Woman* (San Diego: Sparkle Press, 2009).

p. 14, Angie Morgan—with permission of the U.S. Marine Corps Recruiting Command and as quoted on www.marines.com, the command's recruiting website.

p. 15, *Baby Blues*—reprinted with permission. Baby Blues Partnership, King Features Syndicate, ©2011.

p. 15, #10—"Nurses Top Honesty and Ethics List for 11th Year," Gallup, Inc., accessed July 25, 2011, http://www.gallup.com/poll/145043/nurses-top-honesty-ethics-list-11-year.aspx.

p. 16, Did you know?—"Military Experience & CEOs: Is There a Link?" Korn/Ferry International, accessed July 25, 2011, http://www.kornferryinstitute.com/files/pdf1/Military_CEO_Report_FINAL_061306.pdf.

p. 17, Lt. Col. Jerry Carter—with permission of the U.S. Marine Corps Recruiting Command and as quoted on www.marines.com, the command's recruiting website.

p. 19, Ahmard Hall—with permission of the U.S. Marine Corps Recruiting Command and as quoted on www.marines.com, the command's recruiting website.

p. 20, #22—"Military Experience & CEOs."

p 20, Adrian Wooldridge, "How an Expert Took the Lead," *The Wall Street Journal Bookshelf*, accessed July 25, 2011, http://online.wsj.com/article/SB10001424527487039600045754274014310150169.html.

p. 20, Christina Piper—reprinted with permission. Roush and Fernandez, *Heart of a Military Woman.*

p. 20, #24—"50 Happiest Companies in America – 2011," Career Bliss, accessed July 25, 2011, http://www.careerbliss.com/2011-happiest-companies-in-america/.

p. 21, Adam Firestone—with permission of the U.S. Marine Corps Recruiting Command and as quoted on www.marines.com, the command's recruiting website.

p.22, #29—Suzanne Mettler, *Soldiers to Citizens*, product description, accessed July 25, 2011, http://www.amazon.com/Soldiers-Citizens-Making-Greatest-Generation.

p. 22, #29 cont'd—Sen. Fank Lautenberg's biography, accessed July 25, 2011, http://lautenberg.senate.gov/about/biography.cfm.

p. 22, Sen. Bob Dole—review of *Soldiers to Citizens*, by Suzanne Mettler, Oxford University Press, accessed July 25, 2011, http://www.oup.com/us/catalog/general/subject/Politics/AmericanPolitics/HistoryPolitics/?view=usa&ci=9780195331301.

On the Inside | Service Member

p. 24, enlistment oath—10 U.S. Code, Sec. 502 (a), accessed July 25, 2011, http://uscode.house.gov/download/pls/10C31.txt.

p. 27, Seabees inscription—Seabees Memorial, Arlington National Cemetery, Arlington, Va.

p. 27, Frank Schaeffer—reprinted with permission. John Schaeffer and Frank Schaeffer, *Keeping Faith: A Father-Son Story About Love and The United States Marine Corps* (New York: Carroll and Graf Publishers, 2002).

p. 30, Teresa King—Sgt. 1st Class Maurice Cogdell, "The 2010 Power O List," *O, The Oprah Magazine* (October 2010).

p. 31, Code of Conduct for Members of the Armed Forces of the United States—Executive Order 10631, accessed July 25, 2011, http://www.archives.gov/federal-register/codification/executive-order/10631.html.

p. 37, *Broadside Cartoons*—reprinted with permission. © Jeff Bacon.

p. 39, *Fort Knox* comic strips—reprinted with permission. © Paul Jon, dist. by *The Washington Post* Writers Group.

p. 43, *PVT Murphy's Law* comic strips—reprinted with permission. © Mark Baker.

p. 46, LIFE magazine quote—Herbert V. Prochnow and Herbert V. Prochnow Jr., *The Toastmaster's Treasure Chest* (Edison: Castle Books, 2002).

p. 47, Trista Talton, "All-female teams reach out to Afghan women," *The Marine Corps Times* Jan. 9, 2010, accessed July 25, 2011, http://www.marinecorpstimes.com/news/2010/01/marine_fet_010910w/.

p. 49, Rhonda Cornum—"Army Developing Master Resiliency Training," U.S. Army, accessed July 25, 2011,http://www.army.mil/article/25494/army-developing-master-resiliency-training.

p. 50, #180—"The Justice Department Settles with Bank of America and Saxon Mortgage for Illegally Foreclosing on Servicemembers," U.S. Department of Justice, accessed July 25, 2011, http://www.justice.gov/ usao/txn/PressRel11/ SCRA_Settlement_pr.html.

p. 59, *Broadside Cartoons*—reprinted with permission. © Jeff Bacon.

p. 65, Mayra Veronica—"Vice Chairman of the Joint Chief of Staff Brings Encouragement, Celebrities to Troops in Djiboutti," U.S. Navy, accessed July 25, 2011, http://www.navy.mil/search/print.asp?story_id=33564&VIRIN=&imagetype=0&page=1.

p. 67, *PVT Murphy's Law* comic strips—reprinted with permission. © Mark Baker.

p. 71, #274—with permission. Exchange Public Affairs.

p. 78, Nancy Knight—with permission of the U.S. Public Health Service Commissioned Corps and as quoted on www.usphs.gov, the command's website, accessed July 25, 2011,http://www.usphs.gov/newsroom/transcripts/knight.aspx.

On the Inside | Spouse

p. 84, Jeff Edwards, award-winning author of *Sea of Shadows* and *The Seventh Angel*— with permission. Navy Thriller Entertainment.

p. 85, Lisa Black—reprinted with permission. Roush and Fernandez, *Heart of a Military Woman*.

p. 86, SISTERHOOD—reprinted with permission. Debby Giusti, award winning author of ten novels. www.DebbyGiusti.com

p. 93, #320 Jacey Eckhart, "Benefits You didn't Know You Had," *Military Spouse* magazine (July/Aug 2006). www.jaceyeckhart.com.

p. 102, Melissa Seligman—"What A Military Spouse Knows," *Her War, Her Voice!* Blog, February 12, 2011, http://herwarhervoice.com/blog/?p=1313.

p. 110, Theresa Donahoe—reprinted with permission. Kathie Hightower and Holly Scherer, *Help! I'm a Military Spouse ... I Get a Life Too! How to Craft a Life for YOU as You Move with the Military* (Washington D.C.: Potomac Books, Inc. 2007).

p. 133, *Jenny the Military Spouse* comic strips—reprinted with permission. © Julie L. Negron.

On the Inside | Family

p. 142, *Air Force Blues* comic strips— reprinted with permission. © Austin M. May.

p. 138-39, Jill Connett—with permission. Jill Connett, *The Green Plate* (Mustang: Tate Publishing 2008).

p. 150, *Fort Knox* comic strips—reprinted with permission.

p. 160, *Jenny the Military Spouse* comic strips—reprinted with permission.

p. 169, Jennifer Sieracki—reprinted with permission. Vann Baker, creator and owner of MilitaryBratLife.com.

p. 170-71, Melissa Seligman—reprinted with permission. "Strong Bonds," *Her War, Her Voice!* Blog, January 19, 2011, http://herwarhervoice.com/blog/?p=1292.

p. 177, Did You Know?—"Military Brat (U.S. Subculture)," accessed July 25, 2011, http://www.ireference.ca/search/Military_brat_(U.S._subculture).

p. 186, Schaeffer and Schaeffer—reprinted with permission from *Keeping Faith*.

On the Inside | Jargon

p. 201, Schaeffer and Schaeffer—reprinted with permission from *Keeping Faith*.

On the Inside | Traditions

p. 207, Edward Hale—"The Man Without A Country," Vol. X, Part 6: *Harvard Classics Shelf of Fiction*. New York: P.F. Collier & Son, 1917; Bartleby.com, accessed July 25, 2011, http://www.bartleby.com/310/6/1.html.

p. 212, #689—Bruce Rolfsen, "Despite complaints, reveille plays on," *Air Force Times*, accessed July 25, 2011, http://www.airforcetimes.com/news/2010/05/airforce_reveille_ 052410w.

p. 214, #698—Lt. Cmdr. Joseph D. Haines, "Splice the Main Brace: The history of rum in the Navy and Marine Corps," *Marine Corps Gazette*, November 2009.

p. 222, #730—"Welcome to MilitaryTattoo.org," Military Tattoo project, accessed July 31, 2011, http://www.military tattoo.org/.

Outside Looking In

p. 245, Sheryl Roush—reprinted with permission. Roush and Fernandez, *Heart of a Military Woman*.

p. 247, Don Riley—reprinted with permission. E-mail message to military families "back home," April 25, 2010.

p. 248, Tim Hetherington—reprinted with permission. Rob Lewis, "Dispatches from Afghanistan's Valley of Death," *DAV Magazine*, January/February 2011.

p. 274, *Beetle Bailey*—reprinted with permission. King Features Syndicate, © 2007.

p. 278, Caroline Kennedy—*A Patriot's Handbook: Songs, Poems, Stories, and Speeches Celebrating the Land We Love* (New York: Hyperion, 2003).

p. 281, John Schaeffer—reprinted with permission from *Keeping Faith*.

p. 286, #881—Alexandra Hemmerly-Brown, "Face of Defense: Amputee Runs on Inspiration," Army News Service, February 15, 2011.

p. 288, Kristin Henderson—with permission. "Us and Them: Their War," *The Washington Post Magazine*, July 22, 2007, accessed July 31, 2011, http://www.kristinhenderson.com/essays.htm.

p. 290, #893—William Robert Faith, *Bob Hope: A Life in Comedy* (Cambrige: De Capo Press, 2003).

Worth Staying For

p. 296, John Kroger—reprinted with permission. John Kroger, *Convictions: A Prosecutor's Battle against Mafia Killers, Drug Kingpins, and Enron Thieves* (New York: Farrar, Straus and Giroux, 2008).

p. 297, #901—Mollie Gross, *Confessions of a Military Wife* (New York: Savas Beatie, 2009).

p. 299, Salvatore Giunta—reprinted with permission. Elizabeth Collins, "Reluctant hero: Soldier becomes first living MOH recipient since Vietnam," *Soldiers*, March 1, 2011.

p. 301, Mollie Gross—*Confessions of a Military Wife*.

p. 301, Colleen Hensley—reprinted with permission. Roush and Fernandez, *Heart of a Military Woman*.

p. 317, Colleen Hensley—reprinted with permission. Roush and Fernandez, *Heart of a Military Woman*.

Rewards for "Living the Life"

p. 326, Ann Dunwoody—"Q&A: Lieutenant General Ann E. Dunwoody," *Military Logistics Forum*, October 2007.

p. 327, Did You Know?— Elaine Wilson, "Holly Petraeus aims to bolster families' fiscal knowledge," American Forces Press Service, accessed July 31,2011, http://www.army.mil/-news/2011/01/10/50218-holly-petraeus-aims-to-bolster-families-fiscal-knowledge/.

p. 331, Terri Barnes—reprinted with permission. "Blue sky, folded flag," *Spouse Calls* Blog, May 31, 2010, http://www.stripes.com/ blogs/spouse-calls/spouse-calls-1.9571/blue-sky-folded-flag-1.105071.

We hope you enjoyed reading this book and being
reminded of the many positive aspects to military life.
Now that you've jotted down your own memories in
these pages, are there any things you love about
military life that we missed? Please submit them
at our website, LoveMilitaryLife.com. We'd love
to start a discussion on our blog and continue
to add items to our list—well past 1001!

★   ★   ★